WINGS
OVER
LEYTE

Lavinia Bradley

Published by

MELROSE BOOKS

An Imprint of Melrose Press Limited
St Thomas Place, Ely
Cambridgeshire
CB7 4GG, UK
www.melrosebooks.com

FIRST EDITION

ISBN 978 1 906050 11 5

Printed and bound in Great Britain by:
CPI Antony Rowe, Bumpers Farm, Chippenham,
Wiltshire, SN14 6LH, UK

For Roswell,
who made them fly.

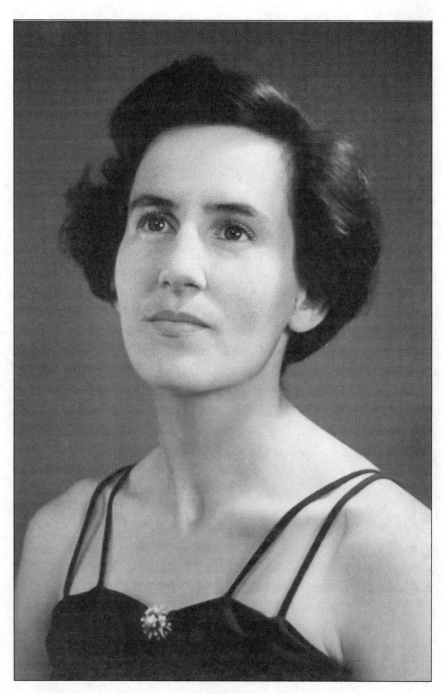

The Author

INDEX OF CHAPTERS

Preface

Illustrations

PREFACE

I have not been feeling myself recently. Given my age and all that I have been through, I imagine I have begun the slow business of dying. This carries an immense sense of responsibility. Being the survivor of so many, and so much, there is a great deal that only I can record. When I go, there will be no record left of happenings that can never be repeated. Only I am left to remember what we saw and did, and how we loved and risked, and sometimes suffered, but gloried in it all. I owe it to my ghosts to set it down while I still can. I am the last guardian of all they stood for.

1

My Destiny Made Clear

My grandmother had travelled the world, following my grandfather into remote and exotic places, where he laid roads, and built bridges and dams, and generally left his mark. Those were the days of the gentleman adventurer, and she did it in style with a retinue of servants. When I told her I was going to Manila, she told me to go to the Army and Navy Stores.

"Buy yourself a parasol and a topee, and always remember in foreign lands you are an ambassadress for your country!"

By that she meant England, not knowing that I was to become an American, nor could she have visualised in any way the sort of world I was about to enter, but I followed her advice and it stood me in good stead.

The time was 1946, and the world had been ravaged by war. There was no civilian transport between England and the Far East. Even letters were unreliable and sent through Army Field Post Offices. The very idea of a young girl setting out on her own was unthinkable, but I had already begun my journey four years earlier when I had met Roswell Bradley, and there could be no turning back.

Love at first sight is questioned but when it strikes it is unmistakable. The French have the words for it – *coup de foudre* –

and that is exactly what happens. You are struck by an almost physical force. When I first saw Roswell – heard his voice – I was momentarily jolted – shaken – blinded to everything and everyone else, as Paul on his way to Damascus – trumpets – cymbals – knowing that I had come face to face with my destiny. After seventeen years, for these few years were my whole life, out of control, without reason or sense, here was my joyous fate. The journey had begun and the rest of my life would depend on him.

Within weeks of our meeting, Roswell Bradley, wartime US Air Force Colonel, had me working in London as a Secretary to top US Army Brass, beginning my education in the US Military, its politics, and its men. We saw the most we could of each other through four years of hard work, and snatches of heady joyous play, bombs and rockets, and our wartime assignments. When peace came, we needed new jobs and his turned out to be in Manila.

There had been a massive buildup of US military equipment in the Philippines, destined for use against the Japanese, but with peace all this material became surplus. It was uneconomic to ship it all back to the US, so the US Foreign Liquidation Commission (FLC) was set up to sell it where it stood. Roswell was appointed Chief of the Aircraft Division for the Far East, with a special brief to foster the creation of civilian airlines. He was now a civilian, but with clout. He would be moving millions of dollars worth of material, and creating communications to a cut-off world.

He had gone back to America to be de-mobbed. Next his telegram arrived:

"GO TO US EMBASSY IN CALCUTTA STOP
YOUR PASSAGE ARRANGED FROM THERE TO MANILA
VIA BANGKOK"

That was it. But how?

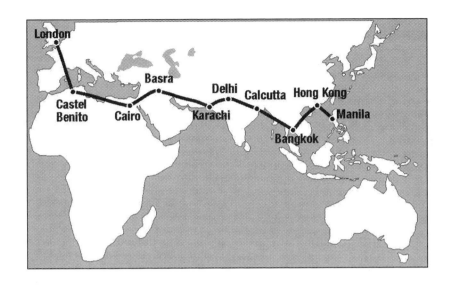

2

THE JOURNEY OUT

India was in the throes of partition, with riots in Calcutta. Anyway, there was no civilian way of getting there. The US Army does the difficult at once, only the impossible takes a little longer. When it meant getting to Roswell, I wasn't going to let it be that long. By a stroke of luck, my godfather was the British Air Minister. I asked him to help me get to Calcutta. To my amazement, in a matter of weeks, I received instructions to board a bus in the Cromwell Road. This took me to an airstrip by a cluster of Nissen huts called Heathrow. In my summer dress, with my parasol, the topee packed into a little suitcase, I weighed in alongside a British Brigadier, a British Colonel, and an Anglo-Indian Sergeant who was carrying a large cylindrical package wrapped in brown paper. We were joined by a Chinese lady, who spoke to no one. Perhaps she didn't understand English.

* * *

On the evening of the 5th of September, 1946, the five of us boarded a small British military plane. It had a series of two seats each side of an aisle. The Brigadier and the Colonel sat together in the front, with the Chinese lady across the aisle. I climbed in, receiving only the customary appraising look and smile given any girl in a pretty dress, and sat behind the Chinese lady at the next window. The Sergeant with her mysterious package was opposite. No one spoke.

Wartime living and its dangers forge a curious bond between peoples. Your mutual dependence upon colleagues, the awareness that life can cease instantly, and how raw it can become in conflict, all contribute an urgency to an interest, if not a sort of affection, between you. It would finally happen with the oddly-assorted four of us winging perilously out of the humdrum of a tired England to unknown territory. I was used to American Generals and Colonels greeting me on sight, but the British at this stage were silent. Our unifying peril was yet to come.

Nor did it take long.

The others were obviously seasoned flyers, and the only instruction deemed necessary was a shout from the co-pilot that our "bags" were in front of us. I looked across at the Sergeant, who smiled kindly and patted a khaki knapsack stuck in the back of the seat in front of her. There was one in front of me too. I smiled back and patted it, but had no idea what it contained. There were also some folded brown paper bags. No one mentioned them.

Our takeoff felt very jerky and undecided. We seemed to go forward, double back and swing round again, then suddenly tipping back rushed madly forward and up. The Sergeant made motions for me to look out of the window, and I could see the lights beneath us very swiftly grow smaller, and then we were on our own with dark outside and the noise of the engine inside, so finally even my tenseness lessened with its monotony. Our first stop would be the RAF Station at Castel Benito on our way to Cairo – then

Basra, Karachi, Delhi, and at last Calcutta where I would find Roswell's instructions.

I suppose I dozed fitfully but proper sleep was impossible. The Colonel kept getting up and lurching down the gangway to what must have been a lavatory in the rear. Each trip he was more unsteady, and finally he didn't even try to hide a flask from which he had been drinking. The plane bucked like a horse and then seemed to drop before rushing up again, and rain began to drum on the windows. The Chinese lady made choking noises, and there was a rustling of paper. She was being sick, and I realised what the brown paper bags were for.

By now I was wide awake. We were obviously in a storm. Lightening flashed all around the plane, lighting us up inside as well. I heard the Co-pilot tell the Brigadier we were going to climb up to 15,000 ft to try and get above the weather, and once again we tipped back. The Sergeant looked across at me and asked:

"You alright, kid?"

I realised by her tone and diminutive form of address that she was showing concern for me, and the Brigadier kept turning around and smiling. Their joint concern alarmed me. Our common peril must be imminent. We were told to belt in and use our breathing masks, and the Sergeant pulled hers out of the khaki knapsack and showed me how to put one on. The ride grew rougher, as we plunged and shook. The engine noise spluttered and changed, and when the Colonel tried to stand up for another drinking trip, the Brigadier restrained him. Nothing was said, but unspoken alarm signals were on and the military unanimously assumed care of me with smiles and assuring looks. We were bonded.

As soon as conditions calmed a little, the Co-pilot came back again and announced that, while there was no immediate danger, we had lost an engine and were returning to Heathrow.

We waited two days before the call came to reboard. The Chinese lady didn't reappear, but the rest of us assembled as best of friends. The Brigadier and the Colonel were all kindness and affability towards me, but, while polite, kept a little aloof from the Sergeant. There was no hard feeling. The four of us were united by our common experience. It was simply the class system of rank within the British Army. But my role had changed from an unknown to their particular charge and responsibility, with due deference to my sex and youth.

It was only then that the dangers of our first abortive flight sunk in, and although from now on it was quite dull and uneventful, I felt a little queasy. As I was to learn later, at the moment of danger you act instinctively and there is no fear. It is only after, when you have had time to analyse the situation, that a reaction sets in. But at the same time I had an added sense of thrill that I was braving all perils to reach Roswell.

Castel Benito was a collection of aircraft hangars set in what looked like endless sand but was in fact hard runway, and we landed uneventfully. Steps were run up to the door and as we went to descend I thought how wonderful it would be to get out of the hot plane, but even hotter air rushed up all about me. It was worse outside. I put up my parasol, and with the Sergeant followed the Brigadier and the Colonel, who were already being met and escorted to the buildings. I must have made a fine sight in my summer dress and parasol in the middle of the spartan wartime operational setting, but all I was concerned with was trying to create a tiny patch of shade.

We were to eat and refuel. There had been only sandwiches and sweet tea from a thermos on the plane. Who knew when we would eat again? In spite of the unbearable heat, we were served large plates of sticky porridge with condensed milk, a thick, virtually uncooked, slab of bacon with its fat still transparent, and a piece of chamois leather the Sergeant pronounced a dried egg omelette, with tinned tomato pulp. There was plenty of thick white bread, and the inevitable ready-mixed tea. The Brigadier and the Colonel seemed to relish it. I thought longingly of US Army messes, and even K rations, but somehow got some of it down.

* * *

On to Cairo over the desert. Clouds formed lovely shapes over the sand which seemed channelled with non-existent streams, rock and sand forming endless dry river beds and tributaries as if mocking its lack of water. I thought of all our war dead down there. What a ghastly place to die!

I now knew Sergeant Bartley's name, and what was in her mysterious parcel. At great inconvenience she was carrying to one of the world's hottest spots, of all things, an oil stove. She was a kindly woman, and, like the officers, had more or less adopted me since our first flight alarm. As we exchanged our particulars, and I told her I was bound for Calcutta, she remarked:

"You must be in love, kid!" How right she was.

We overnighted in Cairo at the Metropole. The Brigadier invited me to dine with him and the Colonel and an RAF officer they had picked up in Castel Benito, and to show me the sights. I accepted with great pleasure. It was not a place to venture into on my own. Even as we disembarked, kites were circling over the officious but inefficient Customs House. The heat, and the smell, and the sheer number of bodies was suffocating. On the streets we were nearly run down by hooting cars, and hands plucked at you from all sides, begging or trying to sell you something. The shops were full of books and shoes and watches and all manner of things wartime England had forgotten. Women were veiled and in black, like nuns, and everywhere disease was openly displayed, usually by thin, dirty, little children, or beggars, blind or limbless, and full of sores. This was my first introduction to Eastern want in the midst of plenty, and it was dirty, hot, smelly and noisy.

But the Brigadier entertained us royally at Shepheards, where we dined with white napery and silver, black-liveried waiters and all the white man's luxury, and then took a bewildering walk through the streets to the famous Tommy's bar for drinks, followed by a snatch of sleep at the Metropole before rising at 3.a.m. to be airborne by 4 a.m.

We were due in Basrah at midday, and Karachi for the night.

I was now feeling reasonably safe with my military escort, when the Brigadier told me they would all be getting off at Delhi.

From then on to Calcutta, I would be on my own. He was quite concerned and suggested that I stay with them in Delhi until another escort could be found. He, of course, knew what might lie ahead of me. But I had no fears. My grandmother knew a retired tea merchant whose firm still operated in Calcutta, and they had arranged that the manager there would pick me up from Dumdum airport, whence I was bound, and look after me until my go-ahead from the US Embassy. What a mercy it proved to be.

Meanwhile, we continued our flight over endless sands, so high we could see the whole of the Dead Sea – desert on all sides right down to the water – and not a living thing. The little I had seen of the Nile at Cairo was very unattractive. The only fertility visible was discoloured green squares and oblongs on its banks. The Euphrates now beneath us was very different. The water was quite green, and its irrigation resulted in rows and rows of graceful date palms. Even the boats looked clean, though the Brigadier assured me they were not. However, our hopes of a break in Basrah were dashed. Due to a political impasse, we were not allowed off the plane and had to sit inside for a couple stifling hours while they refueled, and then came in and squirted us with disinfectant powder. So much for the land of milk and honey.

* * *

Karachi made up for it all. We were to be put up in a country hotel quite a ride from the airport. A military bus took us a beautiful evening's ride into the country. There was no other motor transport. We passed the odd man on a donkey, women in wonderfully coloured saris, often with baskets on their heads, and, to my amazement, a couple leading a laden camel. No one hurried. The dirt road made no noise, and even though it was getting on for evening, the colours were breathtaking. This was the India I had imagined.

Nor did our billet disappoint. The military barracks were not for visiting women, and the Sergeant and I were led through trees and shrubs up to a charming and spacious bungalow, and there waited on by very tall dark servants dressed in white with turbans and red cummerbunds. I imagined this had been the private residence of the Commanding Officer? Or perhaps some private house now annexed for dignitaries, or such as ourselves? We dined in splendour alone in a huge room, with waiters coming and going,. one, especially magnificent, standing more or less on guard by the hot plate. It was so delightful. I was full of smiles and "thank yous" when served my food.

"Out here you don't thank them," the Sergeant told me.

Ambassadress of my country, I had no intention of being rude to natives. Anyway, it is more or less automatic to say "thank you" when a plate is set before you. She seemed excessively stiff and British Army, so I made a point of thanking and smiling against her advice. But by the end of the meal, I noticed the standing waiter was making odd faces at me, which I mentioned to the Sergeant.

"I told you," she said. "You don't get familiar with them out here!"

* * *

Delhi, the next day, was the parting of our ways. The Brigadier was full of fatherly advice and concern, and I realised how much I should miss him. However, at the airport there were small boys selling delicious looking sandwiches, and although the Brigadier had sternly cautioned me against buying eatables from hawkers, I bought one. It was goat cheese. In spite of long waste-not-want-not training in rationed England, I couldn't eat it. Suddenly it came home to me how very foreign my surroundings were. Not even a cheese sandwich was edible. Worst of all, I couldn't speak the language, and the mass of small dark men jostling and shouting through the airport was alarming. I couldn't communicate. But Calcutta lay ahead.

* * *

I had to board a different plane full of chattering Indian civilians, but I buoyed myself up with the thought of the US Embassy with Roswell's instructions awaiting me. In fact my immediate salvation lay with James Wilson from Granny's friend's Gillander's House.

Dumdum airport seemed in a state of chaos, probably its usual state, but so it appeared to me, with people shouting and pushing right up to the plane steps. For the first time my courage waivered; and then I saw a European waving and smiling and realised he had come to collect me. I was so relieved I was near to tears. He had a small old car, and we drove very slowly out of Dumdum to Calcutta, slowly because the streets were almost impassable. They were full of people arguing and gesticulating, some even lying on string beds along the sides untroubled by the traffic or the odd scavenging dog or undisturbed cow. They actually pushed against the car.

"You haven't arrived at a very good time," James Wilson told me, "but it gets better as we reach Calcutta itself. In fact in more peaceful days the Chowringhi, our main street, is almost an Indian Park Lane facing the Maidan, and you'll like Gillander's House."

Gillander's was a haven of peace and luxury. James and another young man, Charles, lived there alone, extravagantly cared for by a large native staff. Hari, the number one boy – actually quite an old man – played billiards with them, after overseeing an excellent four-course dinner, where we sat at a long table, James and Charles at each end with me in the middle. They had been briefed by Granny to try and dissuade me from continuing my journey, but once that duty was over we got on very well. They promised to take me to the American Embassy first thing the next day. That night I slept in peace in my own little island of the old Raj, with Hari lying across the door outside my room.

Here I must digress to explain the rather extraordinary circumstances of Roswell's plan to get me out of Calcutta. At the time, it was a city of violent unrest, curfew and no scheduled flights anywhere, but it was not only India that was in a state of turmoil. The French were battling in Indo-China and now desperately in need of reinforcements. They were looking everywhere for help. Finally they contracted the Dutch airline, KLM, to transport troops into the battle zone, and this was possible in large part due to Roswell.

A team of Dutch officers from Java had been to FLC in Manila, where he had sold them surplus Curtis and Wright aircraft engines and other spares they needed for their C54 Skymasters. Two of these Skymasters were allocated to their KLM airline, flying from The Hague to Batavia. Consequently, KLM were ready to assist Roswell in any way they could, but Manila was not on their route. However, our luck was in.

Reggie Vance, whom we had known as a fellow US Air Force Colonel in London during the war, was now US Air Attaché in Bangkok. Moreover, Reggie had his own Embassy plane and was officially expecting a British VIP he was to fly down to Manila. I had only to get to Bangkok and Reggie could take over. It all sounded very simple but no one could be sure of the timing, or how to communicate with each other.

The RAF had alerted Roswell when I left Delhi. KLM would have a transport coming through Calcutta shortly and, as a great favour to Roswell, would take me on board and make a special stop to drop me off in Bangkok. There I could stay with Reggie and eventually go on with him and his VIP to Manila.

* * *

Next day, James took me to the US Embassy. I was expected. There was a message from Colonel Bradley that there would be a seat for me on a KLM flight which would drop me off in Bangkok where I should be collected by Colonel Vance. While they didn't know exactly when the plane was due, I must be ready to leave immediately. I left my passport and address. They would alert me as soon as the plane arrived. So I went back with James to the last of Raj life at Gillander's House.

In spite of the conditions, James and Charles set out to show me the sights. We dined at the pukha sahibs' clubs, which prohibited dogs and Indians – old England and nothing of India. We fed a baby elephant with rice through a bamboo funnel in the zoo, and made small journeys into safe country, ever with the curfew hours in mind. I loved the colours of the place, but never quite got over my fear of the dark violence and noise of its people in the crowded streets, but my heart wasn't in it. I was restless to keep checking with the US Embassy for news.

Finally word came that a KLM Skymaster was due, would overnight at Dumdum and take off the next day at 5 a.m. The curfew was not lifted until 6 a.m., so an official car would collect officer personnel from the Grand Hotel on the Chowringhi, where I should have to be booked overnight. James and Charles took me to the hotel and fussed affectionately over the booking with instructions for my care. Although I couldn't take my next step towards Roswell soon enough, we were all three genuinely sad to say goodbye. And so I left my last British guardians.

* * *

As soon as their little car had edged away into the crowds, I was approached by a dapper French Army Captain, who introduced himself as the officer in charge of the men I was to accompany on the next day's flight. I was delighted to parade my French, which pleased him, and we sat in the public room for a little while and talked. He was amazed that I was travelling alone, and I was rather flattered by his Gallic attentions and very relieved I had someone friendly to share a language with. He arranged to have me woken, and promised to meet me in the lobby in good time, assuring me it would be his greatest pleasure to look after me throughout my flight. I felt my troubles were over.

Not quite! My room off a long corridor of doors was very small with a high ceiling. There was a fan over the bed whirling three oar-like arms that hummed in a hoarse fashion. The Brigadier had told me never to lie naked under a fan. You must always cover yourself or you would awake stiff. I slipped into my nightie and pulled the rather coarse sheet over my shoulders. Only a few hours and I should be on my way again, but I felt tense – then somehow alarmed. There were raised voices outside the door, and something bumped against it, followed by scuffling and more shouting. Lying there looking up at the wheezing fan, I began to feel very frightened. If we have a guardian angel, mine must have given me a prod. Suddenly, for no real reason, I leapt out of the bed. One arm of the fan flew off, cutting right into the pillow my head had been resting on. It would have killed me. My muscles went stiff with fright. I dressed and sat up in the uncomfortable rattan chair, wide awake and quite unable to relax, until a waiter made my early call. Not wanting to be left alone, I rushed after him through the now silent corridors and into the arms of the surprised Captain waiting for me in the vestibule.

An Indian Army car drove us out to Dumdum, where the Skymaster was already loaded with French soldiers. To my dismay, I saw an ordinary chair set in the gangway – the extra seat put on for me – but with Gallic gallantry, the Captain gave me his window seat and made some unfortunate Poilu sit on it. At last I felt safe. Exhausted by fright and sleeplessness, as soon as we lifted off, I fell asleep. I have always regretted missing the rations they must have issued. French cuisine a l'Armee would have been an experience to compare with US K rations, but after hearing about my night ordeal, the Captain was loathe to wake me and I slept the day away.

* * *

Late afternoon we landed in Bangkok. I alone disembarked. The airport was as makeshift as the Nissen huts at Heathrow. There were three wooden sheds, the largest of which had some chairs and a low table with US magazines on it, but there was no sign of a washroom, and no one spoke English. Eventually I found a Dutch liaison officer, smiling, rotund and fatherly, and asked him if I could find a bathroom. With much bowing and smiling, he pointed to two small raised wooden huts way out at the back in the middle of a field. You entered them by a ladder. There was obviously no running water. However, needs must, so I put up my parasol and self-consciously walked out. It was as nasty as Eastern toilet arrangements usually are.

On my return, the Dutchman had found an English-speaking Siamese official to whom I voiced my instructions to contact the US Military Attaché.

"Ah yes, Colonel Vance – Colonel Vance!" and he smiled broadly and nodded his head and smiled again. He had a musical comedy telephone he wound up but yielded no results. The only advice I got was to sit and read an American magazine. I sat.

At last he told me a party of Congressmen were due to arrive sometime, and although no one could get hold of him, it was understood that Colonel Vance would come out to meet them. Meanwhile, the Dutchman invited me to his room and gave me a delicious meal, mostly rice, but I was so hungry it was manna. Then back I went to my chair to wait some more.

Nothing happened. It began to grow late, and all the Siamese melted away until only the Dutchman and myself were left. He finally said:

"I have to go home. I can't leave you here. You must come with me, and my wife will look after you".

I thanked him but declined. My instructions were to wait for Colonel Vance.

"But he has not come. You can't stay here alone and I must lock up".

"What about the Congressmen?"

"Perhaps they will come tomorrow. You must come to my wife!"

"Thank you, but I can't. I must wait".

It was developing into a panic situation. Then gravel outside scrunched and brakes squealed, and a jeep nearly crashed into the door. Reggie Vance had arrived.

* * *

For me, Roswell was the best looking, and in every other way the most attractive man in the world, but Reggie Vance came a good second. He, too, was over 6ft. with a lean gangling frame, an unhurried lilt to his voice and come-to-bed eyes. He was a West Pointer but, perhaps due to his extreme Southern accent and a slight impediment in his speech, which made him hard to understand if you weren't used to him, he was a loner. Seeing him in his familiar US Colonel's uniform swing his long legs out of a US jeep, I felt I was home. As Roswell had promised, I could let Reggie take over.

He took me to the US Minister and his wife – the Stantons – and we all fell in love at first sight. They were missing their daughter, who was my age and back in America, and welcomed me into the family with almost parental love. And so I entered a new and very gracious world.

3

BANGKOK

Bangkok of the old Siam was still the stuff of myth and legend, and, if feudal and in our eyes sometimes cruel, its people, well-fed in the rice bowl of Asia, were smiling, and rounded and lighter-skinned than the dark, hungry menacing Indians I had left. The Stantons and Reggie were determined I should enjoy it all, and, feeling I was already under Roswell's wing, I set out to savour every moment. Looking back over those few days, I can see they were the only time in my life when I could be utterly self-indulgent. I had no work to do, nothing but respond to the kindness of my hosts in an excitingly novel and magical place.

The US Legation was a lovely house, with high ceilings and much of the woodwork perforated like a doily for air circulation. None of the internal doors came to the floor or met the ceiling. They swung without locks and only covered you from your knees to just over your head to create draught, and, of course, all the windows were mosquito-screened. This wasn't altogether efficient in the bathrooms, where water was kept in great standing earthenware jars for ladling over yourself with a long handled pan. The water would run over the tiled floor and out at one corner, but every time you scooped up a pan from the jar, you raised a cloud of mosquitoes. That night I went to bed in a little white tent of a mosquito net – a house within a house.

Bangkok - Emerald Buddha Temple

Roswell, Bangkok

Inner Court

Royal Tombs

Mrs. Stanton woke me next day, followed by a smiling Siamese girl with my breakfast tray, who, in this land of bright colours, was wearing a ubiquitous white blouse and black silk trousers. I was told this dress was being worn by all Siamese women for a year to honour a time of mourning for the late King – a charming gesture showing loyalty and affection like an extended family, when countries all around were tearing themselves apart.

That first day, Reggie took me to the most sacred shrine in Siam – The Emerald Buddha Temple. Taking a Siamese girl who had graduated from a US college and spoke perfect English as our guide, we entered a world of make-believe.

The temple is in the same compound as the King's palace within double walls. These walls are curved and crooked to keep out the evil spirits they believe can only run in straight lines, and once inside it is fairyland in sight and sound. There is a constant tinkling of bells, only the sound is lighter than a bell toll. It comes from hundreds of tiny gold leaves in the roof gutters that seem to swing in a breeze they must create themselves in the still air. Every roof is patterned with millions of coloured glass or tile inlays, each one separately joined, and all the corners turn upwards, like little curved hands uplifted in prayer – a gesture to the Heavens. The large temple is in the center and all around it stand pagodas. Each time a King dies, a pagoda is built for him, odd pepperpot pyramids of stone, exquisitely carved and coloured, and in and out of them stand strange stone birdmen and dogs and queer figures to guard them. It has no resemblance to our idea of a church. There are no pews, no attendance in the sense we know, no prayer books. Because of the heat, there are no flowers but instead white wax shapes all pointing upward in this gesture you find all over Siam. The statue of the Emerald Buddha sits high up and is clothed differently for each season. At this time, it was in gold and dramatically illuminated way up above our heads. The priest sits on a throne beneath it.

Reggie told me that these priests were rogues. Shaven-headed, they stroll around the streets in orange robes with great black bags over their arms, begging. They literally live off the people and do nothing in return save further the giver's belief that they have done him a service in accepting his gift which will translate into a reward in a later life.

The most remarkable of all is a vast mural painting that runs inside the whole inner wall. Yards and yards long, it is one of the most beautiful things you can imagine. The colour is magnificent, and although it stretches for so long, and must have taken an army of artists in many generations to execute, the style is consistent throughout. It doesn't vary to the extent our Bible does, though the story it tells rambles on and on into deeper fantasy with every brush stroke. Each detail is put in to realistically tell you the story. At one point there is a man being sick (or as our Siamese guide put it "throwing up") simply to illustrate his emotion. The story is told in plaques of verse set all around, some of which she read to us. Their verse is quite unlike ours, and has many complicated forms. It doesn't rhyme. It sings. They chant it in a funny unearthly timbre that only oriental voices possess.

We could have spent all day there but there was yet another treat in store – a royal audience. We were to take tea with Princess Poon. This was living in history. Princess Poon was a granddaughter of a pupil of Anna Leonowen, the Anna of the 'King of Siam' fame. She was the tiniest person I had ever seen, very old and very regal and bejewelled. The servants who brought us tall, thin glasses of iced tea balanced on shoulder-high trays had to fall on the floor within so many yards of her, quite an athletic feat not to spill the tea, and then scuttle away backwards. She didn't speak until they were out of earshot, but then entertained us with such stories of political skullduggery I wondered, with all the royal purges, how the common people ever got out of mourning. Amazingly well-informed, she called all the crown heads of Europe by their Christian names, but she lived in the past with the memory of her father who, except for a short period when she had to attend a queen, had brought her up. She spoke, and seemed to think, like an educated Westerner. However, she had no hope for the present, or Siam's future. She simply shook her head and told another tale of the past, and then with a little flick of her tiny hand and smiling nods, we were dismissed.

* * *

My conception of this fairyland world was soon to be shattered. Next day, Mrs. Stanton took me to see a project near to her heart – the blind school. Buddhists believe any affliction like blindness, or paralysis or any other illness, is a judgment on sins in a previous life. They withhold help or sympathy for fear of bringing divine displeasure upon themselves. Thus, the maimed and blind are neglected, becoming beggars or even slaves.

The Blind School was run by an amazing American, Miss Corfield. This brave old lady, who had such grace and poise you forgot she too was blind, started a school for blind children to try and teach them something other than begging. When she began, prejudice against her was so great, and her premises so often broken into and sacked, she needed an armed guard, but she continued undaunted and could finally dispense with the guard.

"Be brave!" Mrs. Stanton had cautioned me, and I needed to be. It was a heartrending experience. There were twenty-five small children with twitching staring eyes, and some with just dry hollow eye sockets, all with expressions of patience and long suffering. Miss Corfield fed and bedded them with the help of three helpers, and taught them rudimentary English and to make baskets and to sing. One even played a very tinny upright piano.

An entertainment had been arranged for Mrs. Stanton's visit. With one at the piano, they all lined up and sang for us – first the Siamese national anthem, then the US national anthem, and then, most extraordinarily, Loch Lomond. They ended with "All things bright and beautiful", which was more than I could bear. These poor children had never seen anything bright or beautiful. It was too much, and tears started to pour down my face. I looked across at Mrs. Stanton, and she was crying too. Anyway, no one could see us. And, of course, these children were the lucky ones.

The East is fatalistic, but who are we to say they are cruel? They think the Christian religion, that metaphorically drinks the blood of its God, and crucified Him to boot, is pretty gruesome, and if they break their cats' tails to make them better mousers, we cut our dogs' ears and tails for show. Whenever I saw these people they were clean, friendly and laughing. The roads were pits of rubble, but they went bicycling along, or punting down the clon – canal – conducting their business with verve and laughter. Instead of coolies pulling you in rickshaws, they pedalled you in tricycles. They had no running water but they had an Air Force, and the mood was everywhere as relaxed as the girls walking about with a baby slung over one hip, its legs hanging down and looking for all the world like an old belt.

I was entertained every day. I had tea with the American girls who worked at the US Legation, mostly middle-aged career women, who lived together in a delightful house which, if you closed your eyes, might have been in Washington, DC. So we bring our nationhood with us.

There was a memorable dinner at the Dutch Legation, where I encountered my first Eastern meal. Nonplussed at the number of dishes, and being replete after a couple of courses, Mrs. Stanton came to my rescue with imaginative diplomacy. She explained that I was fresh from rationed London, and that lack of food shrunk one's stomach, so I was unable to eat very much. The food was as good to look at as to eat, dramatically coloured with red and yellow spices. One bowl had whole prawns lined around its rim with their pink tails sticking out, and there were endless unknown exotic fruits, from finger-sized bananas to green-skinned, red-fleshed with black pips papayas, mangoes, pomelos and more than I knew. And fragrant, exquisite frangipani blossoms floated in the finger bowls.

After eating, we sat outside in the compound watching fireflies and listening to a woman singing. Their music grows on you. It hasn't really a tune at all. It's a rhythm that symbolised fatality to me, and every now and then the voice skidded up and down like a little wail. It was hypnotic.

Mrs. Stanton took me to dine with some boys from the US Legation whose little house was right on the clon. This is the canal down which life is lived, and trade is punted, day and night. The sampans had families living on them, sampans loaded with fruits or other goods for sale, all bumping together with good humour.

Much as I was enjoying myself, I could but rejoice that time was running out and soon Reggie would be flying me on to Roswell.

* * *

A few nights before we left, a British Regiment who were due to go home gave a dance at the Polo Club. Reggie took me with his party. A great marquee was erected on the lawn, but a few hours later the monsoon broke and the ground fast became a lake. We danced regardless, and the mud never came out of the hem of my best blue dress, but it was a night to remember. Our hosts were mostly young, and one Lieutenant was especially attentive, after all I, too, was young, and fresh and English. Reggie got a little tight – the "where have you been all my life?" stage, so I was glad to have this young officer as a lifeline. His father was a vet in East Grinstead and he was longing to get home. He complained that after a time in the East all the flowers seemed too large and heavy, and he liked them fresh and delicate. He was longing to see a daffodil. It was a night in which everyone was celebrating, which would account for him comparing me to a daffodil. But later, in Shanghai, another Englishman in a moment of nostalgia likened me to a daffodil too, which makes me think it should be our national flower, not just the Welsh. The next night, when I was out, he gate-crashed the US Legation asking for me, saying it was very urgent he got in touch with me. Of course, he was very homesick, and I do hope East Grinstead had a good daffodil crop that spring.

Reggie's official excuse for flying me to Manila was he had a British VIP to take to Hong Kong. Like Roswell, he was a loner and set his own programme of affairs, but that was for the record. I first met this VIP at the Regimental dance, and he seemed anything but important to me. He was dark, stocky and very undistinguished among all the smart uniforms in his safari shorts and jacket. Good manners dictated that I danced with him. He was friendly but clumsy and I rather resented it when he kept cutting in on the much more attractive British officers. He, also, was going home, not to England but to India where he had been born. He told me his father had had a tea plantation but recently he had been murdered by dacoits, and he seemed a rather sad and lonely figure going back to take over. No daffodils for him.

* * *

Finally it was time for the last stage of my journey to Roswell. My evening gown, mudded beyond repair, packed into my suitcase with the as yet unworn topee, parasol in hand, and after affectionate farewells, two of the US Legation girls, the VIP and myself boarded Reggie's little plane and took off for Hong Kong. Throughout the flight, the VIP insisted on regaling me with tales of his life on the plantation – how I would love it – what a splendid way of life – which, seeing he had told me his Dad had been murdered, was not very convincing, until I realised he was trying to sell the place to me. Worse, at Hong Kong, to my consternation, he and I were separated from the others going through the Customs. Their passports were American and ours were British. I assumed that we should be accorded every help and courtesy, but was appalled to see Reggie and the girls waved on with smiles while my trying companion and I were held up and brusquely told to wait. Stuck unceremoniously on a couple of chairs in the corridor, to my utter amazement he begged me not to continue my journey. He would arrange an immediate marriage licence in Hong Kong and give me a perfect life with him on the plantation. Thankfully, at that embarrassing moment, Reggie appeared in full diplomatic force, with a customs official properly contrite at our treatment, and collected us. Later, Reggie was highly amused at what had transpired, but I couldn't help feeling sad for the poor blundering fellow who was so desperately lonely he was ready to beg a stranger to be his wife.

Next day, Reggie and I set off for Manila.

* * *

"Now," said Reggie once we were over clear sea, "how about you having a go at flying us? Come on up beside me and I'll talk you along. Something to tell Roswell!"

Put like that, alarmed though I was, I couldn't chicken out. I climbed into the co-pilot's seat beside him. He demonstrated with a little wiggling just how sensitive the joystick was, and then simply turned it over to me.

I was rigid with fear, and held onto the stick so tightly my hand began to cramp.

"You're doing fine!" he said, smiles all over his handsome face. "Just keep looking where you are going!"

I hung on grimly, though truth to tell there was nothing to see but clear sky over still sea. The instrument needles held steady, and slowly I began to relax, and even enjoy our smooth thrust. Then I glanced at Reggie. To my horror he was asleep. Eventually, with much praise for my performance, Reggie resumed control and manoeuvred the plane to come in low over the dense woodland of Northern Luzon, tipping here and there to give me a better view. Later, Roswell told me that all the time I had agonised at holding our joint safety in my frozen hand, we had been on automatic pilot. Reggie pretending to go to sleep was part of the act.

* * *

We came in on a grassy strip, later to become Manila's International Airport, and took a jeepney to the Manila Hotel. This was one of the few undamaged buildings right on the sea front with the rare facility of a telephone.

Reggie asked: "Where does Roswell hang out? I've got to deliver you fast and get home."

His APO number turned out to be the partially ruined City Hall where he had his office. It was Sunday and there was no one there but a guard. Security forbade him to give us any information. Reggie had to contact the US ambassador's home. Then we got a jeep and set off at breakneck speed through Manila's mad traffic of jalopys, jeepneys and pony-drawn carramatas to Santa Mesa and 113 Valenzuela.

Before the war, this had been a high class district and 113 Valenzuela the house and garden of an English family. Now badly battle-scarred, the US State Department leased it for senior FLC officers. It was a two-storey house entered up wooden steps into a screened verandah that ran across the whole front of the house and into the 2nd floor living quarters.

We passed a great big banyan tree in the drive and skidded to a stop with a great deal of noise, but no one came out. Reggie pushed the screen door open with ease, and in we went. There was only Kali, Roswell's little black dachshund, who noisily greeted us. The place was deserted.

Finally, a round smiling Filipino I recognised at once as the cook, Severo, came hurriedly shuffling out onto the verandah.

"We want Colonel Bradley!"

"Colonel Bradley up country for the day, Sir."

"Damn!" said Reggie. "Well, anyway this is the right house and the right dog. I can leave you safely. We all loved having you. Tell Roswell to bring you over sometime!" and with a hug and a kiss Reggie was off.

With great difficulty I had come halfway across the unsettled world to an empty house.

* * *

Life has its punctuation marks. The day I had met Roswell had been an explosive exclamation mark, setting the entire direction of my life for ever. Waiting for him that afternoon in 113 Valenzuela heralded a new paragraph. Our war years had been fraught with the constant risk of bombs and rockets, but had presented the same danger to us as everyone else. There was nothing personal. Now we were about to enter the most dangerous phase of our lives. The risks ahead, beyond typhoons and tropical diseases and all the common ills threatening everyone, would be personally directed against Roswell and myself.

At last a car drove up. Kali and I tore down the steps and I threw myself into Roswell's arms. There was nothing more in the world I could have desired. I would live for him. I would die for him. And so it would be until the day of his death.

4

MANILA

Manila was once known as the 'Pearl of the Orient'. In 1946 it was a city of ruins. The Americans had had to fight street by street, house by house, to drive out the Japanese, and there was nothing left but a few gutted steel and concrete structures. One of these, formerly the First National Bank of New York, was now virtually a windowless concrete shell and had been made barely habitable to serve as the FLC offices. Without its elevators, Roswell had to climb up five flights of concrete steps – no mean feat in Manilan heat – but once up there had a comprehensive view.

Looking south across the Pasig river, the old walled city of Intramuros was completely destroyed. It had been the site of a terrible massacre of women and children. The Japanese had held out for a long time and were only dislodged by our troops with great difficulty at the cost of its destruction. Further south had been the City Hall, institutional buildings, colleges, and modern apartments and homes of the rich. Now, over 90% of them had been reduced to rubble, and what was left was badly damaged by fire or explosion. On the north side of the river, practically the whole business district had been wiped out, mostly by fire.

But oriental resilience and initiative was unquenchable. The rubble of once modern shops and department stores had

Manila -1945

FLC Office

City Hall

Roswell arriving to launch the first civilian flight

been partially cleared away, and in their place hundreds of one-storey open-to-the-street little tin shacks had sprung up. These plied a noisy good-humoured trade in an assortment of merchandise, mostly native handiwork such as clogs and sandals and reed baskets, and endless liquor stores with dubious labels of 'whisky' and 'gin', and everything was offered at exorbitant prices as a springboard to the game of bargaining that comprises Oriental buying and selling. To shop you needed two words in Tagalog – Magano (how much?) and mahale (too much). After asking how much?, you simply repeated too much – too much – until the vendor, after coming down again and again, finally, with a wide grin, would announce "fixed price!". That way satisfaction was achieved all around. Surprisingly, since we had been to some degree responsible for all the destruction, they showed us no resentment.

* * *

We were reasonably comfortable in our billet in Santa Mesa at 113 Valenzuela, though even here there were reminders of war. During the fighting a shell had exploded in the garden and sprayed into the house, leaving endless small shrapnel holes, and several large ones, on one side wall and the bedroom floor. When it rained, we had to stand bowls and jugs everywhere to catch the water from the roof, and the noise it made was deafening. There were two Japanese soldiers buried in the garden. Roswell found one foot wearing the dark leather split-toed sandal of a Japanese infantryman sticking out of the ground. Only the bones were left.

Another legacy they bequeathed us were the giant snails they had brought with them for food. These had bred in the grounds, and when we drove up the drive at night we could hear the 'pop pop' noise of our wheels going over them as they came out for their evening meal.

From the previous owners of the house, we had inherited comfortable bamboo chairs and sofas for the long screened porch, and our dining table was a pingpong table.

With Roswell and parasol

Gerardo and Severo

113 Valenzuela

We had Severo, a round, smiling, rather dubiously clean Filipino, who surreptitiously fed most of his family, and probably a lot more besides, on our food. We had Gerardo, who was part Chinese, good-looking and highly superior in every way for houseboy, and two lavenderas to do the laundry. All our food came from the excellent US Army Commissary, along with our US Army beds with their khaki mosquito nets, and regulation chests. The Army had put new mosquito screening in the windows. These windows still had their beautiful monsoon storm shutters which, in lieu of glass, had 4" squares of trocha (mother of pearl shell). The grounds still showed a one-time British gardener's touch, in spite of being overgrown and full of papayas, bananas, palms, bamboos and all sorts of tropical vegetation.

With two other FLC officers living with us, I was all ready to go to work and enjoy life. Instead I came down with dengue fever.

Dengue means "bone breaker", and that is exactly what it feels like, compounded by a suffocating fever alternated with ice cold shivering fits, and hot or cold, you are drenched with sweat. Severo and Gerardo changed my bed sheets almost hourly, and for days I tossed about trying not to hear the little gecko lizards who, with suction pads on their feet, lived upside down on the ceilings and in the eves, feasting on the insects that swarmed at night. They chirruped out several hoarse calls at a time, and Gerardo told me that if the calls added up to eight, it foretold death. I was fearful it would be mine.

* * *

Here I must digress to explain the situation of Roswell's mission. The FLC had been formed to sell off US Army surplus left after the cessation of hostilities against the Japanese. As Chief of the Air Division he had responsibility for liquidating Air Force material, excluding actual military aircraft. There were C47s, C46s, L5s, small trainers and others, and enormous quantities of spare parts and such. The action was that the Air Force would declare material surplus on a Surplus Declaration form, which gave a brief description and value. On receipt of this form, together with the minimum price he could charge, Roswell had to sell it on. The minimum price could be as low as 10% of the original value (a C47 Dakota which must have cost well over $200,000 was listed at $20,000). The Government's generous policy was to help its Allies and nearby countries in the area, regardless of price. He could expect plenty of bidders.

There was presently no local air transport. The only air services were American, British, Dutch, and to a small extent French in Indo-China. The Dutch had KLM, who besides helping the French in Indo-China (and me!), were repatriating their nationals from Japanese internment. The British were flying C53s to the Mediterranean, Egypt, India, Burma, Singapore and Hong Kong,

As we were to find out, the China situation was very delicate. Chang Kai Shek, to whom we had already given military aircraft, was our ally against the Japanese, but the Maoist rebels from the West were rapidly gaining strength and advancing in the general direction of the East coast ports, so China was to be handled directly by the US Command in the area.

India was another delicate area. The British and Indian Governments were negotiating partition, and in this agreement all surplus US Air Force property was listed to be turned over to the Government-owned Hindustani Aircraft Co Ltd.

This was a mistake, but the statement citing the non-inclusion of the US Air Force surplus did not reach the authorities in time. This led to a daring and unorthodox solution taken by Roswell and Reggie Vance personally, but more of that later.

On arrival, Roswell had gone out to the PACOUSA headquarters who were to supply him with merchandise, and found them encouragingly helpful.

"Tell us what you want and we'll declare it surplus" he was told. The Air Force had to care for it all until it was sold, and they all wanted to go home, so he could count on their wholehearted cooperation. The aircraft were strewn all around Luzon, but as soon as Roswell could sell them, they would be brought in. So the scene was set.

* * *

Almost upon arrival, Roswell was given a Surplus Declaration for five C47s, and requests for them poured in. Throughout the East it seems there were plenty of people with enormous wealth alongside the terrible poverty. Setting up a local air transport company required substantial finance, but in spite of the war, there were still old families who had survived.

The first call came from Don Eugenio Lopez. He was a small, pleasant Filipino, who had been educated in the US, and with various brothers and sisters owned tremendous properties not only in Iloilo but scattered throughout the islands, dealing in sugar cane plantations, copra producing ranches and real estate in Manila itself. They were very rich. Before the war, they had had a Curtis airplane, which flew from Manila to the islands, which the Japanese had ended. Now he was keen to restart, and even had hopes of one day expanding to make cross-ocean runs. He employed a one-time US Air Force Major, Henry (known as Hank) Meider, to be in charge of this operation. Roswell took to Hank at once, and authorised him to inspect a couple of the declared C47s. Hank found them in flyable condition, and the next day Don Eugenio produced the required certified US Bank cheque of $40,000, the FLC legal man drew up a contract, and they were in business. Hank tore out to Macaulls Field to fetch the aircraft, flew them over to the grassy strip that would later become Manila's International Airport, and had FEATI (Far Eastern Air Transport Inc) painted on either side of the planes' fuselage with PPI designation. Overnight, the word spread that it would now be possible to get to Iloilo in minutes rather than days. Roswell was invited to send off the first flight. A large crowd of would-be passengers were whittled down to twenty-six, far more than a US airline would allow, and along with baskets of pigs and chickens, they took off for a thirty-minute flight. The plane was back in five hours packed with new passengers. The whole operation from offer of sale to operation had taken three days. Everyone was jubilant.

*   *   *

The next move mirrored the first. This time the buyer was a wealthy Chinese, Don Fernando Sycip. He also owned sugar and copra plantations on several of the islands as well as mining interests and export and import businesses He had several of his sons working for him, and also employed an ex-US Air Force man, Lieutenant Colonel Jimmy Lambert. Don Fernando wanted to buy an aircraft as soon as possible to visit his various interests in the islands, and ultimately he wanted to form an aircraft company to give him direct communication with Hong Kong and China. He had ample means, and Jimmy Lambert was a go-ahead type who could responsibly organise such a concept. Roswell still had three C47s. Jimmy selected one, took it out, and the deal was made.

The Sycips lived quite close to our billet in Valenzuela, and eventually we all became friends. Don Fernando's wife was elderly and couldn't speak any English but got on famously with Roswell by gestures and giggles. Neither could she walk properly. In the old tradition, she shuffled about with bound feet – unsightly little lumps encased in ankle-high white kid bootees fastened with dozens of tiny buttons.

Jimmy Lambert had retired to the Philippines and married a Mestiza, (half Spanish and half Filipina). They had a little daughter, Ruthie, and were to become our dearest friends.

*   *   *

Another airline – Cathay Pacific – also started with Roswell's sale of two Dakotas, this time to a tall, good-looking, very attractive American in his 30s Roswell called "the brigand". Roy Farrell was one of the many adventurers left over from the war, trying to make a quick buck in any sort of trading. It was rumoured he had tried his hand at smuggling, trading in imported liquor, money changing, and even possibly the sale of drugs. As soon as international flights started, the greatest demand was commercial to carry goods by hand to Hong Kong outwards, acquiring other things at the other end. Many dealt in foreign exchange, and clubs in Shanghai and Hong Kong were full of stories of huge profits, and losses, and detection of smuggling. It wasn't surprising that the name of Roswell's "brigand" appeared at times as a possible smuggler of opium, star sapphires and pearls, but this one man operation expanded and regulated itself to become Cathay Pacific.

* * *

Both Roswell and Reggie Vance were the most sophisticated of men and yet paradoxically they both had an uncomplicated directness of vision that clarified their thoughts and actions into an almost boy-scout quality of simplicity. This lifted them over a great many obstacles. They solved problems effortlessly by using their initiative and applying the obvious. It was so with the Australians.

Five big Australian airlines wanted planes and spares. The Australian National Airways, Qantas, Empire Airways, ANSETT Airways and Butler Air Transport in all asked for eleven C47s. PACOUSA hunted around and declared eight surplus. Finally, the remaining three were found but only two were serviceable. In Roswell's words, the third was "a load of junk". Its engines had overtime and it needed a great many minor repairs. He confronted PACOUSA, only to find their cooperative attitude had changed. He was told he was to sell what they declared surplus, and only then would they declare more, but not before. It was stalemate.

Roswell could have gone over their head and reported back to Washington but that would further sour relations, so he resolved to fix matters himself. Without further word or authority, he and his officers hunted around and found two Pratt & Whitney engines that had been newly overhauled. They pulled out the old engines and installed the good ones. Next they found a crashed aircraft with spares they could remove and substituted an aileron and a tail plane. Another crash had good wheels and a new undercarriage. In fact, he had them practically rebuild the whole dud aircraft without any further word going out. The Australians were delighted and once again a mission had been completed.

* * *

But it was Roswell and Reggie Vance together who solved a delicate situation with India. As I have mentioned, one of the clauses of the partition agreement between India and the UK was the turnover of surplus Air Force and Army property, which included military and civilian aircraft. The military aircraft did not concern Roswell but there was one outstanding US civilian plane he was loathe to see go. This was a very special plush job the US Air Force Chiefs and US Chief of Staff had had custom built, intended as a gift for Admiral Lord Mountbatten. It was a C47 furnished with all possible luxury equipment. It had a bar, and special entertainment quarters, and was absolutely the last thing in style and comfort, and still being held until the proper time came to present it. Under the agreement, it fell into the hands of the Hindustani Aircraft Corporation – the Government-controlled body – who as far as we knew did not realise it was a special job, and along with others, might be offering it for sale. Physically it was still in US Air Force hands at Dumdum airport outside Calcutta, but Roswell heard from our New Delhi Embassy that Hindustani Aircraft had already had offers to buy C47s, so we were in imminent danger of losing it. Roswell and Reggie hatched their plan. They offered personnel from the US Dumdum Base to take potential customers on demonstration trial flights. Almost immediately, they were notified that a customer was interested and would like to make an appointment for a trial run. What the customer did not know was that a US Air Force Colonel – Reggie – was to be his demonstration pilot. The super aircraft took off, but it never came back. Reggie flew the prospective buyer to Burma, where he offloaded him with the utmost politeness, arranging for his return to Dumdum. Reggie flew via Singapore and Hong Kong to Roswell in Manila.

Here Roswell had had a request from President Roxas for a C47 for his own personal use. Roxas had heard a rumour about something "special". Roswell admitted there was something very special, but it could not be sold at the more or less standard price of $25,000. As President of the Philippines, Roxas was not usually asked for payment, but Roswell explained that this was something like nothing else in existence. The circumstances were unique. It was more of a collector's item. Manuel Roxas was a reasonable man and realised that there had been some finagling in obtaining such a plane, and finally agreed to pay double the standard price. Thus both sides had done well, and Roswell had personally won friendly relations.

* * *

There was yet another Indian adventure Roswell and Reggie pulled off together in the same Biggles-style action. The British had fifteen C47s in their RAF parking lot at Dumdum due to be turned over to Indian hands, all clearly marked with the red, white and blue RAF roundel. While spiriting away the Mountbatten plane, Reggie had ascertained they were not happy about it but were helpless. Accordingly, he and Roswell once more put their heads together and hatched a plan. With British unofficial approval, they took a handful of US mechanics from the US field at Dumdum, gave them some paint, and told them under cover of darkness to paint out the RAF roundels and replace them with the US red, white and blue star insignia. They then drew up paperwork to show that the aircraft had originally been given to the RAF under American/Lease Lend and had now been returned in a reverse Lease/Lend. They were now US property. Roswell was free to dispose of them. Before anyone knew what was happening, Reggie had sold ten to the Siamese Government, and Roswell sold the remaining five in Hong Kong. They had realised $300,000 for the US Government, and resolved a diplomatic stalemate for the cost of a few pots of paint.

* * *

By the time Reggie bought me to Manila, Roswell had already achieved a great deal, and made many friends. However, as is inevitable when the pickings are huge, there are also villains out for the spoils, and an honest man is their foe. Perhaps villain is too strong a judgment. Business practices in the East and in the West are handled rather differently. In the East there is bargaining, and what the West call "squeeze". What the US Government had to offer was greatly sought after, and as the prizes were great, so were the many efforts made to secure them. There had always been plenty of Westerners growing rich in the East accommodating the contenders, with no resentment from the prize winners for commissions they collected. It was all part of an Eastern sale. But as a staunch New Englander, Roswell was un-bribable. At times, with hindsight, it could be amusing, but ultimately it nearly cost us our lives.

* * *

Roswell told me almost his first client had been a villain. Completely disregarding his secretary, he had burst into his office and announced:

"I am Issy Hillman, owner of the Mansion House nightclub!"

He was a large, heavily- built man with a bullet-shaped head sprouting a few red hairs, wearing grubby shorts with his shirt hanging down outside them. He slapped a large cloth bag onto Roswell's desk. Its edges fell apart and a great pile of platinum, diamonds, jewel-encrusted brooches, rings, earrings and such fell out.

"Take your pick," he said.

Roswell was dumbfounded.

"That's right!"

"Do you mean I am to pick out one or two of these articles and they are mine?"

"That's right! Take your pick! I want to get to know you!"

Roswell, man of few words and great control, said quietly:

"Take this junk and get out of here!"

The fellow at once changed tactics, smiled and said:

"I'll explain. Down at the Club we run a wheel (Roswell realised this meant they played roulette) and this represents a couple of night's takings. Rather than convert them, I thought some of my friends might be interested in one or two pieces."

"I'm no friend of yours," said Roswell. "What do you want?"

"I want to buy an aircraft. It's very hard to get liquor, and we use quite a bit at the Club. If we got a good aircraft, we could fly to the US or somewhere where we could buy it, and bring it into the Philippines. We'd use most of it ourselves, but maybe we could make a little by bringing in extra. We could also export Filipino property like copra or something. How much is a good aircraft?"

He kept on trying to buy a C47 but he didn't have the full cash to pay for one. Roswell refused to do business, and eventually got rid of him.

* * *

Soon after he had an even more startling proposal. The Air Force Maintenance and Repair Base at Leyte was to be declared surplus. He was waiting for the inventory and surplus declaration. Various tentative valuations put it at $30,000,000 to $40,000,000 or more, and already he had enquiries as to when it would be offered for bids.

A well-dressed, good-looking man in his early 50s walked into his office and introduced himself as Angel Elizalde. Roswell recognised the name as belonging to descendants of one of the original Spanish families who had acquired great wealth all over the islands. This man was obviously cultured but had an aggressive, arrogant manner. He told Roswell that he had dined with Lieutenant General Whitehead and General MacMillan the evening before. (General Whitehead was the Commanding Officer of PACOUSA – the entire Pacific US force in the Far East.) The General had mentioned the proposed sale of the Leyte Air Base and given him the inventory to take home, suggesting that if he was interested he should talk to Roswell on the basis that a bid of possibly $200,000 could buy the whole business.

Roswell could not believe his ears. It was impossible for him to offer a sale without the surplus declaration, including the inventory, neither of which had he received. He had not seen the inventory. Apparently this man had. General Whitehead had no business authorising anyone to give it to him. General MacMillan had no business giving anyone the inventory without the declaration, though presumably his superior officer had leaned on him. The whole thing was monstrous. It was a flagrant violation of regulations by a high ranking General in sending him a native Filipino with the belief he could offer a bid of some $200,000 for material costing the Government anything up to $50 million.

Roswell explained that material was only sold after being declared surplus, and if there were various people interested, it went to the highest reliable bidder. With great control, he said:

"In connection with this property, I have already had enquiries which will be informed as soon as I receive the surplus declaration. As soon as I do receive it, you will be notified the same as the others. Meantime, I have no interest whatsoever in your bid".

Roswell sent a verbatim report of Elizalde's visit to Washington, but the Leyte drama had barely begun.

* * *

I was still convalescing from dengue when the real drama over the Leyte Base, which was to have such impact on our lives, began. The declaration Roswell received constituted nearly 300 forms. They made a stack 6" high, and showed a total cost to the Government of around $48 million. Endless bidders were eventually whittled down to two syndicates of Chinese businessmen in Shanghai. Each group was represented in Manila by a young American – Ron McCoy and Paul Ranslow. Roswell was unimpressed by either. They were young men with no marked personality, possibly high school level of education and no business experience whatsoever. He guessed they were of the all too common debris left by the evacuating US forces, staying on in the Philippines in the hopes of making their fortunes.

On the appointed day, Roswell and John Stetson, the FLC Commissioner, opened the bids. McCoy for Syndicate A had bid $400,000. Ranslow for Syndicate B had bid $400,001. The closeness of these bids led them to believe there must have been collusion and, on John Stetson's authority, Roswell rejected them both. He would consider a re-bid in fifteen days.

According to a joint agreement, the proceeds of the sale would go to the Filipino Government, so Roswell told the President what had happened. President Roxas asked if there had been any hangars included in the offer. There were two medium-sized hangars of very high grade construction. Roxas told Roswell he would like them:

"When you re-open the bid, leave them out. Offer only the balance."

This Roswell did.

When the new bids came in, there were the same two contestants. McCoy for Syndicate A bid $375,000, which reflected the loss of the hangars. Ranslow for Syndicate B offered the same bid as before regardless, and won.

The next day, McCoy arrived at Roswell's office with two Chinese, and wished to talk to him. Roswell was very busy, and could see no point in any discussion, and had them sent away.

As I have explained, our billet at Valenzuela had a long screened verandah running across the upper floor where we all lived. This provided our sitting and relaxing area. At this point I was well enough to get up for short periods. Usually after supper, Roswell and I would sit there and read or play backgammon, but I still tired easily and that evening I went to bed ahead of Roswell, whom I left reading a book. The bedroom windows opened onto the balcony, and I was settling down when I heard people come up the steps and walk along the verandah to where Roswell sat. It was McCoy with the same two Chinese who had tried to see him earlier in his office.

McCoy led the Chinese to Roswell, and said:

"I am sorry to bother you again, Colonel, but my members have an important message to give you. If you can give them a few moments time, I will leave them with you," and he left.

One of the Chinese spoke faultless English, and Roswell was sure the other understood. They apologised with much bowing and smiling, and the first one said:

"There has been a terrible mistake and we hope you can correct it."

"Go ahead," said Roswell, with little grace, "tell me the story!"

"The bid was incorrect, and we feel we are justified in cancelling today's bidding and reopening it with a corrected bidding. We really meant to bid some $450,000 and $50,000."

"Wait a minute – you mean you are prepared to bid $500,000?"

"Not exactly! Our bid was going to be $450,000, but then there was to be $50,000 for renewing the situation."

There was silence. Then I heard the scraping of Roswell's chair against the floor. I could imagine him drawing himself up to his full height, towering over the two Chinese. I could also imagine the expression on his face. They were asking him to reject the accepted bid so they could submit a new bid higher than they thought the other Syndicate was offering, and for his services in making it possible they were bribing him with $50,000. There was the sound of feet as the Chinese shuffled out, and when they were more or less outside my window, the silent one of the two said:

"It would be advisable for you to accept our proposal. Life out here is different to that in your country. Sometimes unpleasant things happen to people and their families who are disliked."

We had received our first threat.

"Goddamned foolishness!" was Roswell's immediate reaction. It was so outrageous, he didn't pay it any more attention.

The Syndicate B bid stood.

Ranslow had an American friend, "Skinny" Childers, in Hong Kong. He had been shuttling to and from Shanghai, handling the Chinese end of the business for him. When their bid went through, Childers brought down to Manila a Chinese father and son – Powell Khoong and a young man in his early 20s, his son George. The remainder of the Syndicate, possibly four or more people, were elderly men and women over whose wealth Khoong had some control. For the moment, Roswell paid no more attention. There were other things to do.

* * *

An immediate crisis loomed. The Shanghai office were ignoring the rule that vetoed offering military aircraft. They had already declared some small trainer aircraft, and now Roswell heard they had accepted a surplus declaration of twelve B25 Fighter Bombers. This was highly irregular, and he wanted them off the books as fast as possible. He rushed up to Shanghai and told the local US Army group to "salvage" them at once. In US Army lingo "salvage" meant destroy. The accepted method was to use Primacord. It involved winding a thin insulated cable around an aircraft halfway up and detonating it electrically. This cut the plane clean through, completely dissecting it. He was assured the twelve B25s would be salvaged within hours.

The next day, a furious one-star Air Force General burst into his office, shouting loudly that someone had stolen his personal B25 aircraft. He was an Air Force attaché on leave from Tokyo. He had flown down to Shanghai to visit a girlfriend, and when he wanted to return next day and asked for his plane, nobody knew anything about it. It had simply vanished.

Without much sympathy, because of his manner, Roswell had to investigate. Of course, he guessed what had happened. He found the crew at the field who had been in charge of the salvage operation. They had had no difficulty in chopping up the eleven planes in the storage space across the field from the passenger side, but they couldn't find the twelfth aircraft. Finally someone saw it on the other side of the field. It was wheeled over, the Primacord applied, and the remains put on the dump.

What they had not known was that the previous day a Chinese officer, Captain Moonchin from the Chinese Air Transport Command at the Lawan Airport, had heard about the surplus B25s, and wanted to buy one for the Chinese Air Transport Command. The US officer at the field thought it perfectly proper to authorise a trial flight for him preparatory to buying. While the search for the Attaché's plane was going on, and people everywhere being questioned, in came a B25. When it landed, out got Captain Moonchin. He was highly pleased and with a broad smile announced he would buy the aircraft.

The Attaché was far from pleased. His aircraft had had almost zero hours flying time when he took it over. The one Captain Moonchin brought in which he had to accept as a substitute had had almost a thousand. The General was livid and Captain Moonchin was disappointed, but there was nothing further anyone could do.

* * *

It took me some time to get over the dengue fever, but when I was better rather than be idle, we began to look around for a job for me. I had imagined that I should take up more or less where I had left off in London, working for the US State Department in the FLC. They had been liquidating property as fast as possible, with still big deals to come, but the Commission was by this time really acting as a sales agent for the Filipino Government, and already we could see the end of its function. But there was one area, although not really any longer his concern, that Roswell felt needed action. With hindsight I am surprised he could have courted such risk, but of course neither of us had any idea of the dangers. He had dismissed the threat from the disappointed Chinese bidders in the Leyte affair as poppycock. Anyway, being a brave man himself, it would never have occurred to him to buckle under a threat, even had he taken it seriously. St. John said: "Love casts out fear". I am not very brave, but I do know that from the moment I met Roswell, through wartime bombs, raids, whatever, if I was with him I never felt fear, and so it was throughout our lives. He had a wisdom and serenity that always sustained me. Anyway, knives in the back, poison, wire strangling, or any other dastardly threats of the Orient were beyond our conception. We had to accept that Orientals among themselves conducted their business operations differently to ourselves. What Roswell took exception to was that it was the

Americans – Ranslow and Childers – who were cheating. As they started to sell the Leyte property, Roswell began to get complaints of irregularities and suggestions of bribery from their competitors. Bids would be accepted verbally and then later refused for a better bid. They were not conducting business as it should be done. Furthermore, Roswell's office was still handling their affairs as far as FLC was concerned. There were still properties being found which would be declared surplus by the Air Force to be turned over to Leyte Supply. He was loathe to feed a corrupt enterprise. And then he heard they were looking for secretarial help. It seemed a perfect opportunity to nail them. Roswell asked the wife of a Filipino official with whom Leyte had had dealings to approach them with the suggestion that as an expert secretary I might be available to help them out. They nibbled the bait, asked me, and I agreed to join them.

So a routine working background of my life ensued. Each day Roswell drove us to his office in downtown Manila, from whence, for 10 centavos, I boarded a jeepney to take me to the Ranslow house. I returned around midday, and we drove back to Valenzuela for lunch, repeating the same procedure for afternoons.

My journey was quite hazardous. Jeepneys had once been US Army jeeps which were now native owned. They usually had planks put down their sides and centres, and up to fifteen passengers sat, stood or just hung on, inside and out. They competed with each other in garish decoration, painted in all colours, and often with little cotton curtains. The drivers' windows were practically obscured with hanging toys and religious mascots, even vases of artificial flowers. There were no timetables. They were plentiful but unscheduled, and you climbed on whenever you could. They were always grossly overloaded, and drove dangerously fast. Everyone shouted and waved to everyone else on the road in a medley of hundreds of these jeepneys, military vehicles, two-wheeled horse-drawn caramatas, and native driven American cars. After petrol-rationed wartime England, I was utterly dazed, and every ride was a risk.

The Ranslows had a lovely house set back from the hectic boulevard, with the whole front of the ground floor made over into an airy office. I never liked Paul Ranslow, but I worked hard, taking his correspondence and dealing with his Leyte customers – Filipinos, Chinese, Mestizos, Americans and Europeans By the nature of the business they were usually well off, or hoping to be, and they would stroll into the office in the oriental manner prepared to enjoy the barter of a business visit. Ranslow was often out, and I would be entertained by a social call. A little Filipina did the filing, and I was well paid. In many ways it was a cushy job, but the only reason I persevered was that I was acting as Roswell's eyes.

* * *

However, there was still plenty of drama as Roswell continued to wind up FLC business. He was literally changing the face of Manila. In addition to all the aircraft spares and accessories, he had a large quantity of manufactured goods – clothing, food and sundry US Army material to sell.

15,000 cargo parachutes came up. These were coarsely woven in heavy rayon, and came in white, carmine red and a fearful shade of a poisonous green. Within days, it seemed as if all the women and children in the streets were wearing dresses made from them, and the dreadful green colour was the most popular. The material was much too heavy. When the women bathed, with Roman Catholic modesty, they kept their dresses on, scooping water up in tins and pouring it down their neck inside the dresses, and they looked even worse wet.

US Army ration chocolate was another commodity in great demand. Suddenly every street corner had a trader selling it. They would cut the kilo slabs into small pieces and sell them from the curbs of the busy streets. Likewise, Army K rations were broken up and the various contents sold individually, particularly cigarettes. And all this gave employment to thousands, who had no other source of income.

Thankfully nothing to do with Roswell, this happy custom did cause a terrible scandal in China. The US Navy had surplus in

Okinawa, known as the "Okinawa Pile", part of which was the contents of a large hospital ship, much of which reached Manila. There were cotton pyjamas and underwear of the finest US material, medicinal supplies, food, again including chocolate, and blood plasma. This blood had been freely and patriotically donated by the American public in response to a wartime appeal. Somehow this plasma found its way to Shanghai, where it sold like hot cakes from little tables set up in the streets. Understandably, this caused an outcry. Mercifully none appeared in the Philippines.

By fair means or foul, both FLC, and my Leyte customers, were all hoping to make their fortunes, and some used their heads and made a lot of money out of all this surplus. One man bought up all the copper wire regardless of gauge, quantity or insulation at knocked down prices. He even found a lot just lying around in rubbish dumps. He accumulated a vast amount, well over 100 tons, and by some percentage sharing method had it smelted and converted into ingots. He then made his fortune selling them in Japan.

5

SOCIAL, WORK AND INVITATIONS

There was a darker side to all these transactions. South of Manila the Army had what was known as its "Ordnance Pile". Roswell went down to have a look around, and found it was indeed an actual pile of boxes and packages, cans, spare parts, furniture and machine tools. It had no protection from the weather, and only six or eight Filipino soldiers supposedly guarding it. It was strewn about, much of it actually lying in the grass. There were even broken boxes with corners torn off to show what was inside. He picked one up. It weighed around 6–8lbs, and contained four roller bearings of the highest type of engineering accuracy, and undoubtedly cost a great deal to make. The extent of the packaging alone indicated that great care should have been used in handling it, and it was obviously designed as part of some scientific instrument. This sort of waste was common throughout the 'Pile'.

In addition, there was constant trouble from thieves. It all presented an insolvable problem for the Services, who had to guard it until FLC sold it. As soon as it grew dark, robbers came in like a bunch of rats, grabbed whatever they could, and ran off. The soldiers could only challenge them. They couldn't shoot without direct orders.

There was a great deal of ammunition, including aircraft bombs, which he despaired of moving until ingenious natives moved in. They steamed out the amotoll and made imitation detonators which they used to kill fish.

Eventually someone bid a price which might have been an average of $1 in $10,000, and the whole pile was sold in bulk. It was a case of cutting costs.

The evening Roswell returned from the Ordnance Pile he was quieter than usual. He was angry at having seen so much waste from the stupidity of war.

* * *

In Manila's enervating heat, work days found us quite happy to spend our evenings on the verandah. We borrowed the latest US books from an excellent library downtown, listened to good music on a classical radio band and we played backgammon, but of course there were plenty of social functions, official and otherwise.

To break me in gently, our first night out was an informal supper invitation from a young Frenchman, Jean Reldy, who had lived through the occupation and was trying to persuade FLC to give him a job. He and a young American lived very modestly with two Filipina servants in a wooden shack. As most wooden houses in the poorer districts, it stood on stilts against flooding. As we climbed up the laddered steps to the level of the door, we saw the most extraordinary door knocker, but before Roswell could use it, the door swung open. With a sweeping gesture towards the knocker, Reldy informed us that it was the thigh bone of his dearest friend, who had been killed in the occupation.

"If he was still here, he would welcome you with me!"

He ushered us into a tiny room. Throughout the East, the eaves of houses are built low down over the sides to screen out heat and glare, and when the sun moves you are almost in the dark. Electricity, if you have it, is temperamental, so you pump up gasoline lamps, or have candles. In Reldy's candlelight, we blinked. Hanging on every space of wall were native spears and knives, bolos and machetes and daggers. The whole room sparkled from the candlelight glinting on their steel. The Filipina girls served a delicious French meal, over which enormous care had been taken. Reldy made the omelette, and told us the fruit salad – mangoes, bananas, papaya, custard apples, all manner of local fruit – had been soaked in Cherry Brandy all day. He was a marvellous host, regaling us with dramatic tales of the occupation, undoubtedly true, but, as Roswell said afterwards, had lost nothing in the telling, and to top it all, after our meal he produced his pipe whose bowl was carved to resemble a carraboa head. When he smoked it, the smoke came out of its nostrils. In this extraordinary setting, he was gay, charming, amusing, interesting and well read. Even in his Filipino shack there was a flavour of France at its best.

* * *

In contrast, my next dinner party was given by Don Eugenio Lopez, who had been Roswell's first customer, and created the Far Eastern Air Transport Line Inc (FEATI) in three days. As befitted a millionaire, he had a beautiful very modern European-style home at the Elena apartments in Manila. He was a small, smiling Filipino, educated in the US yet retaining the refined manners of his old world. He and his wife, wearing native costume, graciously received their guests. He looked immaculate in a white sharkskin suit worn with a Barong Tagalog – an embroidered shirt made from pina cloth. Pina is woven from pineapple fibre and so fine it is see-through. This was also the basis of his wife's exquisite dress with the high starched puffed sleeves that framed her face like butterfly wings. There were Generals and their wives of both US and Filipino Air Forces, along with civilian dignitaries, mostly from the flying world, all of whom Roswell knew well.

We were ushered through some exquisite nylon mosquito netting onto a balcony. It was so high up it seemed above bugs, and to me faintly reminiscent of Cairo and my evening with the Brigadier. Wine was offered while we sat and talked pleasantly.

Then, rather surprisingly, a soup was served. This was a Filipino speciality with noodles, pimentos and a great deal else in it, and very good. We were then asked to go inside. This was amazing. We passed back through the nylon netting to see a most magnificent buffet laid out.

There was lechon – a whole roast piglet, which is the heart of a Filipino banquet – banana-heart salad made by sacrificing hands of bananas before maturity – adobi (a sort of dough pellet filled with meat) – lapulapu – a delicious native fish here served whole lying there looking up at us with dead eyes – and endless assorted rolls of vegetables and rice. It was a terrific spread, and we walked around it and helped ourselves. It has always amazed me that in the countries of the East where there is so much poverty, where food is accessible there is always too much – not one dish but so many. And this was but the start.

Having eaten as much as we could, we were ushered into another room. Here ladies had to sit on one side, with the men across from them on the other, like a Quaker meeting. Next the Lopez daughters and daughters-in-law came in, very charming and cultured, and handed us more food – Filipino mangoes, Macapoona in a sticky gum, and then Macapoona Surbetes (ice cream) and glasses of champagne. No one left before 10.30 p.m. It was a very grand Filipino supper.

* * *

Of course, the more people I got to know, the more enjoyable such functions became, and the FLC gatherings were fun. General Brown gave a great supper party at the Manila Hotel, gathering FLC members from Manila, Guam and Shanghai offices. He commissioned the whole dining hall to eat in, again too much food, albeit US style. After the meal we went upstairs to a dance floor. This was romantically semi-lighted, and had a hidden band. We sat down a long table and got up and danced at will, but after leading off with Roswell, I hardly saw him for the rest of the evening. He had plenty to discuss with colleagues, and I had plenty of partners.

By the time we came to take our leave, we had hardly had a chance to be together all evening. We made our official goodbye, but once out of the room, Roswell said:

"I've hardly seen you all night!" and taking my hand he gently turned me around and led me back the way we had come. Incognito, we slipped back onto the dance floor and had our dance together. How could I not love such a man?

* * *

The Far Eastern was the other grand hotel in Manila at the time. We were invited there by Major Yuan, the liaison officer for the Chinese Air Force, and his wife.

"This will be a Chinese affair," Roswell warned me. He rehearsed me using chopsticks. "You hold your bowl right up to your face and slurp!" but by the smile on his face I knew there was something else.

"Well, I don't imagine you'll be much good at it," he said, "but after a meal, to show your appreciation, you are meant to burp. Just don't look surprised when you hear the dainty ladies do it alongside their men! And by the way, you'll like the Yuans. We use Christian names socially, and I don't know where they found theirs, but they are called Herbert and Pauline".

Besides our hosts, there was another Chinese Air Force Major and his very plump little wife. She didn't speak English, but smiled and nodded very pleasantly. Her face might have been made from wax, it was so smooth and yellow and shiny. There was also a Chinese Air Force Captain. At the last moment the other American invited was unable to come, but he sent in his place a senior US State Department employee, Annie Dove.

I wore a blue Chinese stiff-collared sleeveless silk dress – a cheongsam Roswell had given me for the occasion to compliment the Chinese women. Annie Dove, who was considerably older than me, also had a sleeveless silk dress, but it was white, beribboned and flounced and trimmed with rosebuds. She was unquestionably from the old Deep South.

In good class Chinese restaurants, a party is never given in open view. Thin wooden partitions divide the floor into little rooms, and each party is ushered into a room of its own, in which there will be two identical tables. One you eat at, and afterwards, in exactly the same positions as before, you adjourn to the other one for conversation. You can hear the other people in the restaurant talking all around you, but you can only see yourselves.

The table decoration is sensibly completely flat. There is no vase of flowers to peer around. Instead, stemless buds and blossoms and single leaves are loosely wired together in a ring and laid straight onto the tablecloth like a wreath, dotted in and out with tiny dishes of sauces, melon seeds, nuts, and all manner of condiments. The waiters wear cloth slippers and silently shuffle in and out bearing countless courses, bent up over the little bowls, nodding and smiling.

The food was delicious and I had no trouble with the chopsticks, but we began with shark's fin soup, and later there was another soup fitted into the middle of the meal, this time bamboo soup, and these I found difficult. We had thick ceramic spoons with flat bottoms like punts, and handles as broad as the mouth, about 6" long and 3" wide, and I found them hard to use. Again it was a case of lifting up the bowl and slurping.

We had a course of great delicacy – duck skin. Another of fish skin and head, parts we would never eat. We had pigeon wings cut straight through the bones, chicken stuffed with lotus seed – again spiky with bones and the seeds like sweet beans, and bowls and bowls of rice with different flavouring. Everything was cut into tiny pieces – really just a taste. There were exquisite little bowls of egg-shell porcelain with weak scented tea, and then lychees. Finally the waiters shuffled round with what looked like great white rolled buns. These were hot towels. Everyone unfolded them, and right there at the table, proceeded to rub their face and necks. They also picked up the small pointed sticks that had been laid out with the chopsticks, and with great delicacy picked their teeth. Sitting beside Herbert, I looked down the table to Roswell sitting beside Pauline, and waited for the belching, but probably in deference to us, nothing happened. Instead, we were ushered to the adjoining table, in the same positions beside the same people for the rest of the evening.

On such occasions, Chinese women are quiet and their husbands make a lot of noise, and yet they are all polite to an extreme. During the meal the men play a game. A man lifts his glass towards a fellow diner, and says "Campay!" which translates "drain your glass". They then both have to drink their glasses dry at one go. Chinese as a whole don't drink, but they will play this game with foreigners, who usually get drunk. To our embarrassment, for all her ribbons and rosebuds, Annie Dove behaved like a man. She talked and laughed loudly, and kept calling Roswell by his Christian name and trying to flirt with him, and to cap it all she joined in Campay. She was vivacious and friendly, but it wasn't only her unfortunate dress that jarred. I was embarrassed for her vulgarity, and felt much more akin to our gentler mannered hosts.

"Don't be hard on Annie," Roswell said later. "Remember our well-mannered hosts are a breed that has practised barbaric cruelties for centuries. Annie may have a loud mouth, but she could never be cruel. Anyway, she probably comes from a big family and has to make a noise to make herself heard!"

6

MAGICAL SUNDAYS

We worked hard all week but Sundays were ours. We had a car and took trips out into the country, had picnics and enjoyed ourselves, and one of our greatest pleasures was driving down to the fishpond country at Iloilo and Bulacan to shoot birds. Roswell found an old double-barrelled Holland and Holland 12-gauge shot gun. It was damaged by salt water near the breech but he easily cleaned it up. He found me a small 20-gauge single shot gun from an emergency kit dropped to lost Air Force pilots, and taught me how to hit a few cans in the garden.

At one time of the year after the rice crop had been harvested there were plentiful jacksnipe in the swampy muddy country where we would tramp for hours. They would come up suddenly, one at a time, and were a difficult shot but very fine eating.

But the greatest treat was when Jimmy Lambert and his friend – a Colonel in the Filipino Air Force who liked to go out with a gun – took us after gallinule, a water bird like a coot, white breasted with green legs, and also delicious to eat.

South of Manila were hundreds of acres of shallow-water fishponds where they farmed little silvery fish that constituted the staple diet of the poorer people. The water was only a few inches deep, and the ponds were divided by clay ridges several feet high

Bulacan - Fishpond Country

Roswell and I

Me

Roswell and Jimmy with the bag

Roswell

Sampan with fishing poles

In the banga

that ran in straight lines, cutting them up chequer-board fashion into rectangles. To shoot, we walked along the top of the ridges, while small boys were recruited to go into the water and drive birds towards us, which would skitter along the water and took quite an accurate shot.

Fishpond country was a good two hours drive South from Manila, which meant an early start. At 4.30 a.m. it would still be dark and relatively cool. Just the two of us awake in a sleeping house bred its own magic. We put on long-sleeved shirts, stout shoes, and took cold cream and topees against the sun, with water bottles slung on US Army canvas belts, ready for safari.

In the semi-dark, the great brown snails left by the Japs were still on their nightly forages down the driveway, and we started out to a cannonade of exploding shells as our wheels ran over them. Once clear of the city, as the light crept up, we could see miles of rice fields on either side, and sometimes over small still water-ditches narrow little stone bridges that might have been in England. Driving through sleepy villages, there was a lovely aromatic fragrance in the air from smouldering smudge fires, lit to kill the pests that attacked the mango trees, and only an odd scrawny grey chicken, or pie dog, about. On those long quiet drives, it was as if we owned the world.

Where the dirt track ended, we would meet up with Jimmy and Luis Reyes. Shouldering guns and ammunition, we walked to the river and banga that would take us the last several miles to fish pond country. The banga was a long dugout canoe, burnt and chipped from Filipino hardwood, fitted with an outboard engine at the stern. We had to sit in line one abreast, fitted into each others bent-up knees, like the stripes of a Sergeant's chevron.

At first, the river was really only a backwater, rising and falling according to the mood of the mother river, without flow to or fro. Only our passage enlivened it, making rough little waves bite and foam at the banks and ripple its green face. On either side, nipa(rush roofed) huts were built right down to the waters edge, each with its banga hauled up onto the mud and untidy livestock – scraggy grey chickens, great black pigs and fighting cocks –

scratching underneath. These wooden huts were raised on struts with their roof and sides thatched with nipa palm. When dry, nipa is the colour of Autumn sea grasses, pale as parchment, and the native thatching left long flat ends waving free, unclipped, unordered and unpegged. And all along the way we picked up chattering small boys who were to be our beaters and gun bearers. As the river broadened, we passed smaller bangas paddled by a man or boy sitting in the stern, the length of his canoe in front of him laden with earthenware pots arranged in single file right up to the tip and filled with fish for market, or flat round baskets of bananas or rice. Only the depth of his craft would save him from being tipped over by our wash and sending all his merchandise overboard, but there was no ill-will, just shrieks of laughter. We also passed strange fishing rafts suspending long poles tied one onto another that supported great black nets for dragging fish, and on each one was a nipa-woven tent that was home to a fisher family. Here and there, great nets like snow ploughs were planted in the mud to catch more fish.

As the river widened, we left behind huts and banana trees and vegetation. Gradually the world transformed itself into miles and miles of flooded land raised from the river bed itself and squared into watery fields by the mud dykes, too shallow for the banga. The boatman tied it up to a pole, and we disembarked onto a dyke. We kept a small boy each to carry our ammunition, and later to retrieve our shots, while the rest splashed chattering into the water like a Sunday school treat.

The dykes were broad enough, but we went single file, Luis leading Jimmy, and Roswell next, with me close behind him, and it was hard going. The mud was often imprinted with caraboa hoof prints that the sun had hardened into rocklike pits. Other creatures had thrown up heaps of mud that had hardened into stone, and my steps were too short to fit into Roswell's long strides. I also had to carry my gun broken – bent in two – as the safety lock was too stiff for me to work, and it grew heavier all the time. On we walked for miles under scorching sun until the head beater gave the signal to stop and spread out along the dyke. With the sun up, the reflection from the water was intense, and we covered our faces with the cold cream and the water in our bottles was tepid and metallic tasting. It was a moment to look around.

Far away, on the blue mist of the horizon, we could barely see the open lips of a mountain volcano but all about us the world was flat and water.

Soon, from a little way off, we would hear the chatter and calling of the boys in the ponds, slapping the water with sticks and throwing mud. As they got nearer, the birds would start to fly, and they would yell:

"Brato! brato!" which means wild duck, and "gallinule!", the bird we had come to shoot and as our guns started, we put up the odd white heron, which would rise in a graceful lolloping flight against the blue of the sky, and local painted snipe, but what we wanted were the black, green-legged water birds with white on their breasts – gallinule.

The one bird no one touches is a boceye. Roswell told me that in America they were called "shit poke" because they had a nasty habit of voiding a steady stream of waste body matter on takeoff.

It was rather different to potting cans in the garden at Valenzuela, but I was determined to do my best. Our first day out, an awkward bundle of feathers, legs, and a long neck rose up almost on top of me, and I shot it. Immediately all the boys began to cheer and laugh and throw themselves about, and I felt great. But what I had bagged was far from game. It was, of course, a boceye, I still think such a small target as its thin neck was a fine shot, but I have never lived it down.

As the birds fell, the boys beside us would jump into the water to retrieve the floating bodies. They would string them by their necks onto a beaded cord like a rosary. Each wooden bead had a double string passed through it, the head of the bird went into the loop and then the bead above was pushed down to hold it firm. My poor boceye was left to slowly sink.

After a stand, we would walk on and repeat the whole procedure. Each time it was thrilling – the rush of the boys splashing and calling – the birds suddenly coming over us from nowhere –

trying vainly to keep up with the other guns – and all around the extraordinary watery flatness under blue, blue, hot, hot, sky.

* * *

One Sunday, Jimmy's three Mestizo brothers-in-law came with us. Mestizos were white natives, remnants of the original Spanish invasion from which the country still takes its religion and in part language. This time we went by Bulacan instead of Iloilo. At Iloilo when the tide was low the banga grounded in the mud, so we were forced to drive further to a broken bridge where the river widened. At halftime they took us to a deserted hut and fed us. They gave us prawns the size of lobsters, and tiny crabs, to shell in our fingers and dip in a sauce of raw vinegar, which were delicious, but followed by cups from a bowl of dirty looking water in which a fish had been boiled whole and still looked up at us with dead white eyes.

We were all shooting for our larders, but the real reason the Prado brothers came was to inspect some fighting cocks en route. Americans joke that Englishmen love their dogs more than their children. I am sure Filipinos value highest their fighting cocks. Thousands of pesos change hands during cockfights. Fortunes are made and lost – lives too, and not only those of the cocks. It is all taken so seriously that the owners often risk a knife in the back from a jealous opponent.

The hens are skinny little grey birds. The cocks, of course, are coloured, but for all the care lavished upon them not much bigger. When you enter a village, you see them tethered by a string and peg, and they continually leap against the fetter, the idea being this will develop their leg muscles. The men constantly handle them, carrying them around under their arm, or squat in the road or pathway and pull at the string to exercise them. They stroke their sinewy thighs which are usually plucked, either from recent combat, or done by the owner to give freer movement. Each district has its central arena where fights are held, and they are reputed to be bloody and to the death. Sharp double-edged blades are fixed to the birds' heels that deal a merciless cut. Oft times a fight can take just one fatal jump.

The Prado boys wanted to enquire about a cock at a rice farm outside Bulacan. The rice had been cut and stacked in ricks that looked like the heads of washerwomen, round and topped with a knob, but we left them to negotiate the road in their jeepney by themselves. It had great rocks laid on it that hadn't been dug in, so the car tipped up and down, murdering the tyres. But we could see palms on either side, and the nipa huts with women bustling about carrying rush trays on their heads, but surprisingly without grace due to their heel-less wooden sandals. They had cross straps at the toes, often cut from old tyres, and unless they clenched their toes with every step they fell off. It made an ungainly gait, but they waved and laughed. They wore a sort of shapeless slip that hung low on the breast and back from shoulder straps and must have been beautifully cool in the heat.

Driving home was like seeing an old black and white film in colour. The rice fields of the early morning dark were now bright green. According to the season, their colour would change. Young rice is almost saffron and it grows to a deep sea-green in maturity, turning hay-like after life.

Coming into Manila, we would pass an amazing Chinese cemetery that spread over an acre or more of land. Every noted Chinese family in the city had a small stone temple or shrine there in which to bury their dead, and the more important the family, the larger the burial ground. Later we were to become experts in cemeteries, and, as with Stonehenge, we would always marvel at where all the grey stone came from. In the Catholic cemeteries there was a lot of cement, but the Chinese, honouring their ancestors, had the real stuff.

* * *

Another activity that gave us great pleasure was an evening expedition to the movies. In spite of its ruins, Manila had made up a splendid movie house that showed all the latest American films with lurid posters all over its facade. Each week, as the programme changed, we drove to downtown Manila and lost ourselves in Hollywood fantasies. The Bob Hope and Jimmy Stewart films entranced us, as we'd met them both in wartime London, but what we enjoyed most was the US Cavalry saving the brave frontier folk from Red Indians led by Jeff Chandler as Cochise or Geronimo. Childish perhaps, but Roswell's mother was a DAR (Daughter of the Revolution) which brought history near, and we were in the East much as those early settlers who had gone West. And to finish the evening, welcomed by a large cardboard Polar bear at the door, we would go to the El Dorado Ice Cream Parlour for Macapuna Surbetes.

Every so often, coconuts throw up a freak. Instead of milk in its center, it has a semi-solid gelatinous viscous middle – and this is macapuna. It is greatly sought after, and quite delicious, and we would compete with each other in finding the rather rare solid pieces in our ice cream.

After the FLC sales, when local buyers broke up the US Army rations into small saleable parcels, there were small boys running all over the city with trays hung around their necks, chirping like noisy little birds proclaiming their wares, and one of these was a sugar-coated spearmint chewing gum that came in little rectangular cubes called Chiclets.

One evening, enjoying our ice cream at the El Dorado, Roswell kept finding large pieces of macapuna in his dish, which he teasingly displayed. I had none at all. Finally, after a lot of ribbing, I did spoon up one piece and jubilantly bit into it, only to find it tasted of spearmint. With unashamed glee, Roswell waved the remnants of a Chiclets wrapper at me. He had, of course, been slipping them into his dish all the time.

* * *

Filipinos did not keep pet dogs. There was always the odd scavenging pie dog sniffing around garbage dumps, or anywhere else they hoped to find food, but they were not pets. People were finding it hard enough to feed themselves without useless animal mouths, and there was always the very real threat of rabies. The only dogs we heard of were those owned by the Igorot tribes north of us in Baguio, and these were bred for eating. The meat was reputed to be rich. It is really no different to breed dogs than it is to breed sheep or pigs to eat. The only nasty side to it was their method of killing. They beat them to death. This was thought to tenderise and enrich the flesh by releasing glandular excretions – repellent to Western thinking.

The servants thought our love for Kali, the little dachshund bitch Roswell had brought back from Delhi, extraordinary. No one else kept a household dog. And then we heard that another American, Chick Parsons, also had a dog, and what was more, it was a male dachshund. At once we decided to breed them, and at the proper time Honeyboy Parsons came to stay with us.

That weekend we made up a picnic, and, with the two dogs, drove out to Tagaytay. There, Ipo had a great concrete dam and reservoir that supplied Manila's water, and during the occupation this had been a Japanese stronghold. It was an exciting, wild drive through much uncultivated country with plants and trees strange to us, but as we passed the dam we saw the pathetic sight of rows and rows, seemingly for miles, of white wooden crosses marking graves of fallen US soldiers. There must have been as many young men from Japan scattered about nearby, just as dead and all far from home.

The dam was a great mass of concrete, and there was a welcome breeze off the water of the reservoir, but the level was low in its great bowl of scrubby land. While we sat under a tree on the rim to enjoy our food, the two dogs tore up and down the sides barking with joy. Whenever we ventured out into the country, we seemed to be the only people in the world, but this time another car came up the road and stopped. Out got a couple, obviously amused by the dogs. They came over to talk to us and he introduced himself as an English official of Shell Oil and he and his wife made themselves very pleasant. We shared our coffee, and by the time they went on their way we had sealed a bond of friendship with a promise that they should have one of the puppies in due course. And so we met the Sanguinettis.

Honeyball went home to his master, and Kali began to incubate her first memorable litter. And here in the writing of accounts must come parentheses, for amongst all the other events that would follow, Kali and her puppies would be responsible for friendships, and the saving of one, as well as the tragic losing of another human life, all to be part of our history.

* * *

Those Sundays were magical. It was pure joy to be alone together, and exciting to explore a foreign land. We were cautioned about driving deep into the country by everyone content to hang around the Army and Navy amenities. The Hukbalahap – Huks – were reputed to be still active, particularly in the country, hostile to Americans who backed the Government. These people had helped fight the Japanese but were now the opposition to the Government, and branded as villainous Communists swinging their machetes at all opponents. There also might be small pockets of forgotten Japanese. We never found anyone unfriendly. The nearest thing to seeing an enemy was a US Army truck with a handful of dejected Japanese soldiers someone had found hiding out in the backwoods being driven into Manila.

When the rice paddies had been flooded for planting, we drove North towards Los Banjos and saw a white carraboa. Carraboa were working all day in the rice fields, ugly fierce-looking animals with very small boys sitting on their backs yelling and kicking and whacking them in complete control. Seeing a white one was like finding a unicorn among carthorses. They are very rare and valuable as they can go longer than normal ones without water. These great creatures have to spend at least five hours a day wallowing in muddy pools. That day was the only time we ever saw cattle. There was a small herd of Indian cows on a Bureau of Hygiene reserve with humps on their backs like camels.

Another time we made for Los Piñas to see salt gathered. On the way were bare spidery trees, thin and tall and almost leafless that hung with great fat round pods. These were Kapok trees. The pods turn from a dark green to brown, and then burst scattering the kapok like thistledown. Once it was a thriving business, used for lifebelts, and mattresses, and cushions and such, but the cost of gathering and transporting it on a regular basis was too high. The locals still took a little into Manila when they felt like it, but they eventually lost out to foam rubber.

Passing through Los Piñas there were crude wooden signs with 'ASINI23' on them. 'Asin' is Tagalog for 'salt'. Soon, as the coast came into sight, we saw nipa huts with sacks and sacks of salt piled up behind them. Reminiscent of the fishponds in Bulacan, there were enormous flat square trays of sea water evaporating in the sun. It was already growing late. After the hot day's sun, men were out in the trays with large wooden rakes, combing great white piles of salt from the tray bottoms. Salt that we, and the rest of the world, had been eating all our lives. If I had ever thought about it, it was sea, or perhaps tears, diluted and invisible, but here was the actual stuff being raked into mountains.

* * *

"And now," said Roswell, "on our way home I want to take you to meet Joe Arcache."

We stopped at a beautiful old Spanish stone house on Tanduay Street in Manila, and were given a royal welcome by Joe Arcache and his whole family. The house was exquisite with narra flooring, and entirely panelled with Philippine hardwood. It was full of children milling around Mrs. Arcache, who was heavy with her ninth baby, but my attention was riveted on Joe Arcache himself. Improbable as it was, Joe Arcache was Jewish, rather small but so dynamic you could feel energy in the air around him. He was reputedly very wise, and very brave. On one wall was a citation of his spying activities during the Japanese occupation. He took us up to it, and remained very quiet as we read it. Among many feats, the citation gave an account of how he had swum the Pasig river to get information about Fort McKinley. When we had read it, he said:

"That cost me two sons!"

He told us that when he got back, he found his wife in the throes of a premature labour brought on by anxiety, during which the Japanese, who had some threads of suspicion, burst into the house. They knocked Joe about badly, trying to make him slip up and give himself away, and the baby was born dead. His little 3-year old son saw all this happening, crawled up behind one of the soldiers, and bit him in the leg. The man swung round and catching the child by its legs flung him against the wall until his head cracked. At this point in this dreadful narrative, poor Mrs. Arcache burst into tears and rushed out of the room.

He also showed us a radio they had kept hidden behind their toilet throughout that was never found. In all, they lost three babies in the occupation.

* * *

Sundays, and life with Roswell generally, were magical, but I soon began to dislike the atmosphere in my office. I personally had nothing to complain about, but I began to pick up instances of mismanagement by Ranslow and his friend Skinny Childers that disadvantaged the syndicate they were meant to handle for the Khoongs. Talking to customers, and prospective customers, and putting together various details, I was sure there was a system of double bookkeeping, which could only work to the disadvantage of the Khoongs. Of course, the customers were all out for a bargain themselves and many not too particular how it might be arranged. They were usually well off and able to take a chance but one day when Ranslow was out, a thin, rather pathetic, fellow came in. For some reason he excited my sympathy.

Gus Dodds was an American/Filipino trying to appear all American. Dressed in long white pants and white shirt, already crumpled in the heat, he told me he had a Filipina wife and seven children. He had no job, and was hoping to buy from Leyte Supply and re-sell to advantage. He was, of course, completely out of his depth, and fair game for Ranslow. Checking the files, I found double entries. It was disgraceful to cheat anyone, but somehow worse to hit anyone as vulnerable as poor Gus Dodds, so, without actually saying anything, I laid both sets of accounts on the table and left them for him to see he was being double-crossed. Poor Gus Dodds brought my findings to a head, and I was ready to report to Roswell. Roswell agreed that there was enough evidence to inform the Khoongs as to what was going on, but he was too late. The poor Khoongs were in terrible trouble.

* * *

We had negotiated with Chang Kai Shek's people in Formosa (Taiwan) for engine spares. Another Chinese consul also enquired about cost and availability of certain propeller parts. We had submitted a quotation and delivery date, and received an official order from the Consul. The parts were shipped and Leyte Supply was paid. It was a substantial sale and we were very pleased. However, shortly after, George Khoong was with some of his friends in Nanking who had been on the receiving end of the material, and they complained to him how costly it had been. George found that they had paid 35% higher than our actual price. Innocently, he remarked:

"It seems that you've been taken for a ride. You paid for more than we quoted."

His friends immediately reported this to the Chinese in Manila, who were furious at being caught out. The finger pointed directly at the Consul, who, in his turn, wreaked vengeance on the poor Khoongs for having exposed him. They were arrested on a spurious charge of having traitorous business with the Maoist forces, and after many months in prison in Nanking were deported to Formosa (Taiwan) for fifteen years' hard labour. It was a completely trumped-up charge. Roswell approached everyone he could, but to no avail.

We are bought up to believe that the mills of God may grind slowly but ultimately justice will prevail – right is might – but this is strictly a Western concept, and in the East an optimistic one.

Buddhism actually teaches that the only certainties in man's life are death and sorrow – happiness is a transient treasure. There would now only be death and sorrow for the poor Khoongs.

The Khoongs had had the controlling interest in Leyte Supply. Their friends rallied around to carry on its affairs and eventually asked Roswell to be their representative to make sales and contracts on a 15% of the proceeds basis. He was so enraged at the treatment of the Khoongs, who were no more red than he was, that he agreed.

This all came about at an opportune time. To our great joy, I found I was expecting a longed for baby, and although Roswell's time with FLC was ending, we wanted to stay on in the East. We were full of plans, and this Leyte Supply connection would be welcome.

* * *

Roswell's accomplishments in FLC had been enormous. He had disposed of hundreds of millions of dollars worth of Air Force surplus, fulfilling the needs of millions of people who had been without imports for four hard years. He had helped grounded air lines fly again, and created new ones. Selling US Army surplus consumer goods, he had made employment possible for countless Filipinos, from wealthy merchants down to street hawkers. And he had realised over $3,000,000 from aircraft sales, and $4,000,000 from spares and tools for the US Government. Washington, DC, let it be known that:

"No other FLC field office made such a comparable record in the disposal of aircraft property".

Roswell was pleased, but characteristically remarked: "Well, no other office had so much material!"

* * *

From the President down, he had made friends. It wasn't only me that fell under his spell. And yet he was a very reserved man, quiet enough to disguise the fact that he didn't suffer fools, or

67

knaves, gladly, but it wasn't only gallinule that were despatched by his sure shot. His aim was sure and unswerving in all ways. He had a touch of ruthlessness that earned Eastern respect, but it was always made acceptable by a gentle humour. It is rare that Orientals truly accept Western races into their hearts, or even homes, but they genuinely liked Roswell. And he had gone out of his way to get to know Filipinos and Chinese outside office enclosures. Sundays had taken us far beyond the boundaries of our colleagues and we had met all kinds of people in friendship. In April, 1947, his job accomplished, the Manila office closed.

* * *

The US Air Force retained a skeleton staff at Nichols and Clark Fields, but the US Government lease on our billet at Valenzuela expired on 1 April. Roswell announced:
"We shall have to find somewhere to live!"
These were golden words to the next paragraph in our lives. It felt almost dangerous to be so happy. Here I was in an exciting country with my beloved Roswell, our baby in the making, and the dogs – Kali and Dickon the puppy we had kept from her first litter – to have a home of our own. However, initially the reality wasn't very romantic. The divide between rich and poor was enormous, and we had no Governmental aid. A primitive hut jammed into a downtown street like Jean Reldy's hardly appealed. We found an advertisement for a little house on Maganda Street. 'Maganda' is Tagalog for 'beautiful', so off we went to find it. The directions took us into an unsavoury section of the city. We drove down a muddy track with wooden shacks on either side, and all the other native sights of hens and pigs and dogs and bare-bottomed babies. We continually stopped and asked for directions to Maganda Street. No one had heard of it. Finally, at the far end of this slummy place, we saw a broken wood sign stuck in the mud. This was 'Maganda Street'!

* * *

And then we had a piece of luck. Another FLC couple, Bill and Melba Cunningham, had also elected to stay on in the islands. Instead of being with us in the billet at Valenzuela, they lived outside Manila in a native barrio. This barrio was the usual group of nipa huts but there were also several small houses, and they rented the upper floor of a two-storeyed American style wooden house. It had been built by a Master Sergeant, who, after the Spanish American war in the 1900s, had married a Filipina woman and settled. He had built a small raised bungalow in his garden facing a lane which still bore his name – Sargento Mariano. Bill found out it was empty, partly because it overlooked a Catholic cemetery which the locals feared at night. It was offered to us at a reasonable price, and we were thrilled to accept.

Leaving Valenzuela was no problem. We only had our clothes and dogs to move. As always happens, when the US Government decides to pull out, it simply closes and leaves the native help to fend for themselves once more. Doubtless they are all well paid for their services. Our lavendera, who had tirelessly washed and ironed to perfection, I had never seen. Severo, our cook, had also given good service. Middle-aged, like many of his generation pitted with small-pox scars, he was round and giggly and ever-smiling with reason. We had been his gold mine. His son, Ignacio, limping from childhood polio, cleaned our shoes, stealing anything he found left around, and Severo more or less fed his family and friends from our back door. Our going would hit him hard, but I didn't feel much sympathy for him.

But Gerardo was different. He had been our houseboy, waiting at table, cleaning the house, dealing with all eventualities. He was a good-looking boy with Chinese blood – his surname was Tan – and before the war had worked for an English family. They recognised his value and taught him their ways. When they were interned by the Japs, he risked his own life smuggling them food. When they were rescued and repatriated, they had recommended him to their US liberators. Now he was to be abandoned again.

Our future was exciting but very unsure. We were in no position to engage a houseboy. The time came to leave, and Gerardo put the dogs into the back of the car and stood back. We warmly shook his hand and thanked him. He bowed his head, I suspected to hide tears. I felt full of emotion myself. We got into the car and looking into the car's rear mirror could see his forlorn figure standing there, watching us leave. We looked at each other. Then very slowly, Roswell got out and went back to him. He asked:

"What are you going to do?"

"I don't know, sir!"

"Well, understand I can't employ you but you can come along with us until you decide what you want to do."

And so the three of us, with Kali and Dickon draped over Gerardo's knees in the back of the old blue Pontiac, drove out to our new home.

* * *

One of the reasons we had elected to stay on in the island was Pete Miles. Pete was an American known as an "old Filipino hand". He was much older than Roswell and had been in the Philippines long before the war, working with the Inter Island Steamship Co. They had handled personnel traffic and baggage goods and had been very profitable. Then the Japanese came and he was imprisoned. He was taken across the inlet at Corregidor and held for a time near the Pacific coast, then force marched North and interned in the infamous Los Banjos camp. Here, amid unspeakable hardships, Pete became a legend.

Towards the end, when the Japs were under pressure, they had planned to simply starve the camp out. By the time the US Forces had reached Manila, there were only two days rations left. Somehow, with great courage, Pete, and two other old-timers who knew the island, managed to escape and reach the Americans. As a result, our US Forces sent boats into Laguna Bay, and then dropped parachutists right onto the camp. Pete had made them a chart with the position of every Jap sentry marked on it, and the Americans picked them off one by one and liberated the camp in one morning. The inmates were pitifully weak from hunger and disease, but the

Americans managed to get them into the boats waiting in Laguna Bay and had them safely in Manila before the Japanese main forces knew anything about it.

For years after, ex-prisoners told tales of how, not only then but continually, Pete had risked his own life to help the sick or others in difficulties. But to look at, he was an unlikely hero. He had skin like leather, and beside Roswell he looked like a little goblin with twinkling blue eyes. He was completely unpredictable, and in the orthodox sense semi-literate, but he had an inexhaustible knowledge of local flora and fauna, and he was a great romantic.

When we first met him he had a vast laundry that took in ship's laundry and hotel stuff. We saw sheets being ironed on great mechanical rollers run by ancient machines running off even more ancient generators, but now the enterprise was going, Pete had grown bored and put it in charge of the largest negro I had ever seen – Mr. Lefty – of whom we should see more. Pete had moved on to a new dream. Full of enthusiasm, he told Roswell about Palawan.

7

PALAWAN

Palawan is one of the extreme southwest islands of the Filipino group, long and slim, roughly 50 miles long but only 2 miles or so wide. It was so thinly populated by Moros as to be virtually uninhabited, save for a penal colony on the western side, a leper settlement, and the one small town of Puerta Princessa. The island was one of the richest sources of natural resources in the whole group, covered in virgin forest and entirely undeveloped. Pete told us of huge trees of valuable hardwood, mostly Apitong – a dark red-brown timber with the grain and appearance of mahogany. His dream was to form a company to fell these trees, move them to the coast and load them onto some kind of ship to market them in Manila. There was a desperate need for hardwood for beams and rafters to rebuild the ruined city, and the quantities on Palawan were huge. If successful, with such a certainty of demand, there would be substantial profit. And there would also be sidelines of crocodile skins, almasiga (gum copal), parrots, cockatoos, orchids, beche de mer and birds' nests (for the Chinese), rattan, and sica and mangrove firewood – a cornucopia of exotic tropical products. It was heady stuff listening to Pete's accounts of a sort of Swiss Family Robinson and Robinson

Crusoe rolled into one. It seemed all nature lay waiting for us for the picking.

Perhaps it was the lure of country untouched by man after the ruin and desolation of war, of which we had seen so much, or an unconscious memory throwback to forbears who had settled untrodden land in New England, but Roswell was hooked. He certainly had an interest in trees and the chance to build an occupation to augment whatever Leyte supply would bring was very appealing.

Pete had no money to put into anything speculative, but he had extensive practical experience and close friends in useful places, like the men running the Luzon Stevedoring Co. Roswell had no money to invest either, but he too had goodwill and contacts from the President down, and was eager to learn. He could be a very valuable associate.

* * *

There were only two sawmills working in Manila, both owned by Chinese. By a stroke of luck, the Dee Chuan Co was run by Robert Dee, son-in-law of our old friend Alfonso Sycip who had bought one of Roswell's first DC3s. He offered all his help and took us over his workshop. They were cutting great logs with a circular saw, and the whole yard smelt of the sweet sappy smell of newly-cut timber.

"We have a city to rebuild," he told us, "and we are desperate for hard timber." All he could get was a semi-soft wood from Northern Luzon called Luan. It came in two varieties – a plain luan, cream coloured like pine, and red luan which had a pink tinge. Both were cheap and plentiful but their use was very limited because they were so soft. Could it be got, he estimated it would take at least ten years to satisfy Manila's hard timber demands.

The more Roswell looked into it, the more appealing the project appeared. He got books from the Bureau of Forestry, and we read up everything printed about Filipino hardwoods. The exotic names of Ipil, Dao, Kamagong, Narra and Palopsapis, with all their properties, rang like poetry in our ears, and they were all to be found on Palawan.

Of course, it was a romantic dream – a remote island with no roads or development – probably insurmountable problems of labour, harvesting, transporting, always coupled with the trying heat of tropical conditions – the question of gaining the permit to form a company at all – but the magic was the flavour of those days. Enchantment won over reason. The tropics hold plenty of dangers – fevers and ulcers, mosquitoes and leeches and spiders, and always the heat – but it intoxicates, and at that time we were drunk with its magic of a fairyland island. Even our baby was coming. And so we took up residence in the little barrio of San Rocque. This was not just a new paragraph. It was a fresh chapter in what was to become an adventure.

Our new home – Binagbarilan corner of Sargento Mariano – was a very small raised wooden house at the end of a dirt track, facing the Municipal Cemetery. In Europe it could have passed for a child's playhouse. It had a dusty yard with a big mango tree, a kianito (custard apple), a papaya and two tired banana trees, and was fenced rather unsteadily with wire from the native barrio sprawling all about it. At the back there was a cement platform with a spigot for laundry. Roswell drove the car in underneath the house. We all got out and climbed a wooden staircase at the side into a little mosquito-screened verandah across the front. This was our first home.

We both thought of the Wild West movies we so enjoyed – the pioneering couple cut off from civilisation with only the basics to build from. This was the Wild East. I looked at my sophisticated Roswell, and he looked at pregnant me, and we laughed with pure joy.

"I guess we'll have to do without the US Cavalry if we get into a fix," he said, "but it's going to be great!"

It was terribly hot, and we could smell pig food and garbage piled up in the sun a few hundred yards off on a pig farm. The house was filthy, but we couldn't have been happier.

Roswell had done a little horse trading over furniture with colleagues returning home, and Pete's friends from Luzon

Stevedoring lent us a truck to deliver two US Army iron beds with khaki mosquito nets, and a regulation swivel mirror dressing chest. They barely fitted into the tiny bedroom. We also acquired a double rattan chair which furnished the verandah and a couple of chairs for inside. To top it all the truck offloaded a giant 7ft petrol-run refrigerator, which was put under the house along with the car, which Gerardo in short time made over into his own quarters.

But the nucleus of the whole house was a gift from Robert Dee of Dee Chang Trading. He gave us an exquisite little table. The whole top was one piece of a rare hardwood with a superb grain – Tangile. Roxas in his Malacanan Palace could offer no finer.

Our little home was ideal. We owed a great deal to Gerardo, who translated for us in the barrio and taught us the local tricks and customs. In return, he lived with us in his own little domain under the house, and we realised his dream of going to La Salle College in Manila. He was gone in the day, but he waited on us in the evenings and did odd jobs at the weekend. Life very quickly became a double drama. I was finding the heat very trying with the baby weighing me down, so gave up my job to find living in the barrio an adventure on its own.

* * *

Meantime Roswell and Pete were trying to make the Palawan dream come true. The problems were immense. How could they move felled trees down to the coast through dense forest? And if they could, how would they ship them to Manila? It was a Roswell/ Reggie Vance sort of scenario. However, before long he and Pete devised an ingenious idea of fixing an overhead cable over the felling operation to run down to the coast. With wheeled trolleys carrying large sharp tongs that opened up to 10ft to grip a log, with a pulley arrangement to lift them off the ground, they could then run timber down to the sea.

Ironically, FLC had already solved the shipping question. Luzon Stevedoring Co had lost ships to the Japanese in the war and

Barrio San Rocque, Pasay, Rizal

Our home

After the typhoon

The cemetery

Caleb and Magnesia

Me in barong tagalog
(pina cloth made from pineapple fibre

in compensation the US Government had given them several surplus US Army TLCs (Tank Landing Craft). These boats were made to run up onto a beach, with large doors in the bow that lowered into a ramp. Palawan had a sloping beach and the lowered doors would be ideal for loading logs.

Pete recruited a crew of men and was ready to go into the forests and start cutting trees. We then found that without a timbering concession – the official Filipino Government permit – he could not touch a single tree. Concessions of any kind in any field were rarely granted, and then only with the highest political influence. It was stalemate. Pete went out and got drunk.

Roswell came quietly home.

"Don't worry," he said, "I'll find a way!"

Knowing his inherent tact and charm, coupled with his understanding of Eastern manners, I had every faith he would.

Next day, Roswell met a young Filipino friend who was the personal aide for social affairs to President Roxas – Ping de Leon. They exchanged pleasantries. Ping asked him what he was doing, and when Roswell told him suggested he approach the Minister of Agriculture, Don Juan Rosario.

"But," Ping cautioned him, "on no account ask for help over a concession. Merely show a personal interest in forestry."

Roswell made the appointment and liked Don Rosario at once. They talked at length about US birds, particularly waterfowl which were one of his interests and for years had been one of Roswell's too. They hit it off handsomely. He next asked Roswell his impression of how industry might develop in the country after the war, and what prospects there might be? It was some time before he brought up the subject of timber operations. By then it was evident that Ping had spoken to him.

"I understand you know people interested in a possible timber operation on Palawan. Are they serious, and could they make a good thing out of it?"

Roswell assured him he had the highest respect for the Luzon Stevedoring Co, and liked and trusted Pete Miles, the titular head of the project.

"And what is your particular interest?" Don Rosario asked.

Roswell said he hoped to have some part in the project, as he dearly wanted to stay on in the Philippines. This seemed to please Don Rosario, who politely closed the interview saying he had knowledge of Roswell's work over the past two years and wished him all success in future plans. He made no remarks whatsoever as to the reason for Roswell requesting the interview.

A couple of weeks later, Ping told Roswell that President Roxas wanted to see him. He greeted Roswell by his first name and asked about the timber project he was interested in.

"I haven't much time but tell me about it!"

Roswell was as brief as possible.

Roxas listened, and then remarked how much he enjoyed his "fat cat" C47 which Roswell and Reggie Vance had spirited away from India. The interview was over.

"Darned fool way of going about things," Roswell proclaimed, "you talk about everything but the matter in hand!"

But very shortly, Pete and two top Luzon Stevedoring men were summoned to Malacanan. They were presented with a licence signed over the national seal of the Philippines to a 3-mile square concession on Palawan, allowing them to cut and ship up to 40,000,000 cubic metres of timber, with the proviso that the Government took 30 pesos per cubic metre removed. It was much more than we had hoped for.

* * *

While Pete and his friends were celebrating, Roswell came home to our own joyful occasion. Kali was in the throes of delivering her second litter of puppies. Five arrived quite normally, but suddenly something went wrong. It seemed she was trying to expel a further puppy and it was somehow stuck. She became very ill.

"We need help!" said Roswell. He wrapped her in a blanket and carried her out to the car. What help existed, I couldn't imagine. There were no vets in Manila.

Roswell drove straight to the US Army hospital, and with Kali in his arms, asked for help. Within minutes, the whole hospital staff seemed involved. Nothing like it had ever happened before. A top US Army surgeon took a small dachshund into the most up-to-date, lavishly equipped Army hospital, diagnosed a dead puppy in her ruptured uterus, and performed a hysterectomy. Her uterus was bottled in formaldehyde to be kept on show. Medical history had been made.

Kali survived, but we had to feed her pups with a medicine dropper every couple of hours for quite a while. Two of the little brown bitches were absolutely identical and we were always getting confused as to which one had been fed, so to distinguish one from the other Roswell put a dab of milk of magnesia on the head of one we thereafter called Magnesia. She grew into an extraordinary little dog, who later played a life-saving role in our family.

But the story of Kali's operation resulted in a terrible ending. Several weeks later, a US Air Force officer took his sick dog to the hospital hoping he too would be helped. Tragically, the dog bit the surgeon in his groin, and he died a dreadful death from rabies.

* * *

With the timber concession granted, it was action stations. To date it had been planning work. Now, tools and supplies had to be shipped, labour recruited, the cable arrangement for getting logs to the coast built, and a bank loan negotiated. Pete and Roswell, with a well-schooled young Filipino clerk, took a small office in Manila and began to activate the Miles Timber Co.

Luzon Stevedoring shipped off a TLC to Palawan for the first load. Pete had sent fifteen men to the island to fell enough trees right onto the shore to make up the first shipment. The boat ran into the shore bow first, let its ramp down, and the first tree was pulled on by tractor, lowered into the bow lengthwise. The first difficulty was that the trees were of different lengths and diameters, so we lost a lot of space. There was practically no deck room and all the logs

Unloading the first shipment from Palawan

had to be loaded into the hold. In the end the load was nearly 100 tons short of the original estimate. Still, we were very excited. A month from receiving the concession, the first shipment arrived in Manila.

The Dee Chuang Co had agreed to buy it, but first there had to be a customs inspection. This meant a visit from a Filipino official, a bottle of drink and 50 pesos for his checking the manifesto. He looked at each log by number and estimated its weight. Then the Dee Chuang manager looked over the cargo and agreed to pay the suggested price. We had managed our first load and the ship should have turned around and gone back for another, but we were learning the hard way. With the wastage of space in loading the logs, it was ridiculously uneconomic. We had to find another method of transport.

Finally, it was decided that the wooden barges used for loading sand and gravel would work, but barges had to be loaded lying in the water. We should have to build a pier, and that meant time and money. Pete found a floating pile-driver, but had to rebuild its engine before sending it down to the island. Luzon Stevedoring supplied a floating derrick. We also needed a great deal of sawn timber for decking and furnishing a pier and had to find a sawmill with a generator to provide it. It was the summer of 1947. With luck, it would be complete by October.

* * *

No one was idle. Roswell worked at making valuable sales contacts, resulting in promises from Shanghai to take as much Apitong as we could supply.

Pete found the US Army had 230 Personnel Landing Craft no one wanted. He made a very low bid, and was accepted. Some were in very bad condition, but the real hitch was they were strewn all over the islands. They had been run into small inlets along the coast and drawn up onto beaches. They were all over the place and quite a problem to find. He decided the only way to handle them was to scrap the boats, take out the engines, and overhaul and sell them for as much as he could get. He sent out search groups to bring them back to an empty garage in Manila. Filipinos make excellent mechanics. They overhauled them in groups of twelve, and Pete started to sell them at 2,500 pesos – a fraction of a new engine. Then Roswell got a handsome overall bid from Hong Kong. The deal ended with a fine profit that helped defray the cost of the pier building costs.

* * *

By late summer, pile-driving for the pier had matured and so had our baby. We had put off going down to the island until the project was well underway but when I was within ten days of expecting the birth, we could put if off no longer. As a freelance, Roswell no longer had a plane at his beck and call, but after a word with Jimmy Lambert and Don Ferdinando, they offered us one of their C47s to fly us down. We were up at 5 a.m. and drove to Makati airfield by 6.45 a.m. It was another of our magical drives through a half asleep world, this time full of excitement. At last we should see, not only what we had been working on for the last few months, but the wooded island of Pete's dreams. A friend, Ed Murray, was to pilot us, with a Filipino for crew, and we took off on what promised to be a gorgeous day.

In its US Army lifetime, the Dakota had been "a workhorse". This one hadn't changed much when it became a civilian for CALI (Commercial Air Lines Inc). It still had bucket seats – iron benches down the sides so you faced the passengers opposite. In my condition it was very uncomfortable, and we had many flying hours ahead, but Roswell sat next to me, and, with a typically sensitive gesture, held my hand, and I would have sat on hot coals for him gladly.

But an hour or so along, Ed told us we were in trouble. Our left engine was overheating and we needed to land as soon as possible. We were passing a small forested island, and running up from the shore into the trees was a narrow clearing of rough ground. With great skill, and a few shuddering bumps, Ed put us down. It didn't take Ed and the mechanic long to find we had burnt out a starter, and couldn't possibly go on. We had finished our water and sandwiches, and it was fearfully hot and uncomfortable.

Mercifully the radio was still working, so while Ed contacted Manila for help, we climbed out and tried to shade ourselves under a wing. It was too low to stand under, and as soon as we tried to sit down, which was uncomfortable for me, ants made us miserable. Ed finally got a signal that a plane from Zamboanga on its way to Manila would pick us up, probably in six or seven hours. It wasn't very encouraging.

Of course, our arrival had been noted, and very soon friendly locals began to appear, and our mechanic relayed to us an invitation to go with them for shelter. We gratefully accepted, and the four of us were escorted by smiling guides along seemingly random paths through banana and papaya trees giving way to more serious forest. The procession grew larger as we went, joined by excited children, until we came to a cluster of nipa huts. My pregnancy was very popular among the women, but presented quite a problem when we saw the entrance to the huts was a bamboo ladder. Roswell had to more or less boost me up. Inside, the floor was made of narrow bamboo slats on which they squatted. They gave under our weight whenever anyone moved. A box was found for me to sit on, and our hosts giggled and chattered and did their best to entertain us. The worst part was gracefully accepting their food – a far from clean looking mess of rice and yams and something fishy – but Roswell ate most of mine for me.

Six hours later, the rescue plane arrived. It was, of course, much too late to land on Palawan, but they agreed they would fly us over our timber operation on its west coast before the long haul back to Manila. It was wonderful. We had upholstered seats to sit on and windows to look out of, and the passenger in the seat opposite me not only had an enormous revolver with a mother-of-pearl handle sticking out of his back pocket, but painted fingernails. Nothing was any longer unbelievable.

Palawan lived up to Pete's description. There was virgin forest for miles and miles, with trees going right down to the sea edges. Here and there were golden beaches bedded with white coral running into clear aquamarine sea, and endless little atolls. And winding in and out of the tree mass you could see the glint of a crocodile-infested river caught by the sun. We flew low, and could just make out the half-finished pier sticking out into the Pacific. There were a few small clearings of fallen trees, but otherwise the entire island was completely covered with dense primeval forest. As it began to darken, we flew into a glorious tropical sunset of vibrant greens. I was so exhausted I no longer knew where reality and sleep divided.

In Manila, Jimmy Lambert and a handful of friends rushed out to the aircraft to meet us and were most solicitous in handing me down to earth. Once safely on my feet, Roswell and Jimmy clapped each other on the back.

"My God, Jimmy," said Roswell, "I've never been so scared!"

I thought this most odd from a man who knew every sort of danger, until I realised they had all been apprehensive the baby would arrive. And more moving still, Gerardo had voluntarily missed his schooling. Of course, the dogs gave us an hysterical welcome. I felt very cared for.

* * *

As soon as I had known I was pregnant, Roswell had taken me into Manila to see a legendary "old Filipino hand", Dr. Fletcher. He had been practising years before the war, probably the only American doctor. When the Japanese came, like Pete, he was incarcerated in the infamous Los Banjos camp, where he too had saved countless lives. He was still practising from a little office in downtown Manila against more showy, younger competition. He was a bespectacled small man, now elderly, quiet with a gentle manner, and at once I felt complete confidence in him. He sympathetically summed up my situation – a young girl in foreign parts and climate, with stars in my eyes but no female backup – and knew, of course, that at the moment of birth the sweetest romance becomes a harrowing experience. After he had examined me and forecast a date to expect the baby, he said:

"My dear, all should go very well. Just remember that everyone in the world has been born!"

After our Palawan trip, we went from day to day expecting the baby. Roswell rather reluctantly resumed his usual pattern of going to the Manila office, coming home for lunch and a brief siesta before an afternoons work, but he was edgy. When he was away, I was completely alone in the barrio without any communication at all.

I had written to my friend, Elizabeth, who had had four children, to tell me what to expect at the onset of labour. It all seemed quite straightforward, but nothing happened to me. I went eight days overdue. On the ninth day, I woke up with a pain but according to Elizabeth's letter it was in the wrong place, so I insisted that Roswell went to work. I still had the pain when he came back for lunch, but nothing had changed, so I sent him off again. But then, right place or not, the pain grew really intense, and I realised I was in labour. Roswell had only gone a few miles, but he was so uneasy he turned around and came back. I was ready with my bag packed.

The Clinic was a good hour's drive, and most of the road our end was unmade, full of potholes and bumps. It was a terrible drive. There was no doubt the baby was on its way.

We finally reached the Ayala bridge over the Pasig river. The Clinic was the other side. It was late afternoon. The bridge was crowded with jeepneys and right in the middle, jamming the traffic, two had collided. Their drivers had got out and were fighting each other right in the center. We could actually see the Clinic, but couldn't reach it.

Roswell looked so white he might have been having the baby. He got out of the car, pushed his way through the jam to the fighters and somehow got it across to them what was happening. Eventually they made a channel through for us and we got across.

The entrance to the Clinic was a long corridor with straight-backed chairs along one side. Roswell put me on a chair and desperately sought help.

A little Filipina nun came and asked me:

"First baby, missus?" and when I said "Yes", she assured me with smiles it would be a "long time", and disappeared.

As luck would have it, Dr. Fletcher was in the Clinic. I was put on a trolley and rushed off. Wherever it was they were taking me, I never got there. We turned into a side room and I began the serious struggle to finish giving birth.

Possibly an hour later, Roswell was called in. I was still on the trolley, and a nun showed him a little bundle of blue blanket. Inside was our first son. Roswell smiled down on me on the trolley – our love – a new life – Heaven itself can never better that moment.

* * *

When we left Valenzuela, Roswell had given me two books – 'The Good Housekeepers Cookbook' – put out by 'Good Housekeeping Magazine' – and 'Dr. Spock's Baby Book'. From these I was to learn cookery and baby care. My ingredients and situation were rather different to that of their usual reader, but they did me proud. As far as the baby went, it was really just common sense.

Roswell and Gerardo built what could have doubled as a meat safe for a crib. It was a wood frame holding mosquito screening on legs, each of which stood in a can of water against termites. The lid lifted up to put the baby in. Gerardo had given him a rush-woven mat for a mattress. It was perfect.

We also had a pair of baby scales, a canvas bath and cool cotton Birdseye diapers. We were all set.

Caleb never gave us any trouble. We treated him rather like a parcel, picking him up and putting him down, taking him with us wherever we went, but of course initially we curtailed our country excursions and stayed in the barrio getting to know him. And life in the barrio was never dull.

* * *

We looked out onto the Municipal Cemetery. It was like having a front seat at a Gilbert & Sullivan operetta. Although ardently Catholic in the most garish way, a Chinese influence had crept in with tombs and stonework. We looked down on red-robed and blue-robed Madonnas and nuns, with stone faces painted like prostitutes. There were endless white, or bright pink, cherubs clutching flowers, all from the same mould, perched on engraved stones, and often under elaborate little roofs were framed photographs of the grave's occupant with "Ala Ala Ng Fmakia" ("Remembered by his family") inscribed in lurid colours.

Funerals were noisy entertainments. Announced from far off by a brass band playing a Hawaiian Love Chant, or Auld Lang Syne, in slow tempo, the coffin would arrive in a jeep converted into a hearse by hanging dirty white cotton curtains at its sides. All along its way, it collected followers, with a good number of small boys chewing gum and popcorn to the encouragement of more who flocked out from the barrio to join the fun.

As the coffin was lowered into the ground, the relatives shrieked and wailed, and tried to throw themselves on top of it. We watched it happen so often, and it always followed the same pattern – an accepted ritual.

But once the coffin was interred, the jeep turned around, everyone fighting to get on, or hang on, and the band, playing the same two tunes now jazzed up the tempo and turned the occasion into a gay parade.

* * *

The cemetery had its true heyday on the Day of the Dead – All Saints Day. Several days before, there was a general tidying up, shooing out runting pigs and poultry. Traffic would be diverted up our lane and on through the pig farm out onto a road again. Gerardo, always well informed on local barrio events, announced:

"Candles will be lit, and feasting will go on all night in memory of the dead!"

This meant a lechonada – the Filipino celebration on any occasion entailing the roasting of pigs.

On the day streams of jeeps and pedestrians filed into the cemetery all day long. We watched from our verandah, and when evening came it was a charming sight with candles dotted like stars at every tomb, and little groups of people at each stone. It was hard to believe it was a cemetery. A small market had cropped up inside the gates, largely manned by our neighbours from the barrio behind, who had seized the opportunity to make more money in an evening than they did otherwise all year round. They had gathered every sort of fruit and vegetable and were boiling great pots of rice, running what amounted to a restaurant service. Small boys ran in and out, jumping onto grave stones and off again, shouting their wares – popcorn and Popsicles and ice drops. Tables had been set out for gambling games. Their attendance was phenomenal, and some accepted lumps of melted candle wax, pilfered from the tombs and still warm, as currency. Further in, couples were courting in and out the angels, and for a fee priests read a prayer over a grave, making money like everyone else. It was stifling with the heat of so many people and the candles, and the smell of the pigs up the lane hung overall, but it was a vast party, business better than usual, and never a wet eye.

Roman Catholicism, introduced by the Spaniards, had been embraced with fervour and lent colour and drama to their lives, providing an excuse for an on-going party. Every Saints day was elaborately celebrated, and each barrio had its own patron saint who rated a parade. In the bigger towns these were magnificent affairs. Religious images were carried shoulder-high through the streets, lit with candles and festooned with coloured paper on makeshift thrones, like dolls sitting on birthday cakes. There was Our Lady of Fatima, and the Virgin of Antipolo, and when the Black Nazarene of Quiapo – an effigy of a negroid Christ – was paraded, people were trampled underfoot and seriously injured in the fight to touch it to gain its healing powers. Devotees in rich costumes mingled with ragged bare-bottomed boys, all carrying lighted candles in the tropical heat. A brass band blared out music with nothing hymnal about it, and the priest in his black skirts was shaded from the sun by a small acolyte holding a great black umbrella over him.

The Saint for our barrio was San Roque, the protector from dog bites, and small boys threw stones at our dogs when the procession passed our gate.

All the schools were run by nuns. Every major street had an ornate Spanish-built stone church, however poor the surrounding houses, and everyone made the sign of the cross passing them. On my jeepney trip to the Ranslow office, I saw a man cross himself with one hand while he picked the pocket of the person sitting next to him with the other. Even criminals were caught with gold crosses and holy medallions hung around their necks.

The peak of their religious year was not Christmas but Easter. This seemed very logical to me. After all, birth is universal. It is resurrection that is not granted to common men, but here everything changed. Throughout Holy week, there is a hush over social life. Even the movies close unless for a religious film. Then on Good Friday, all hell breaks loose. In the Filipino interpretation, a religion of a loving God with kindliness as a prime virtue changes into one of barbaric cruelty and self-torture. Barrios stage realistic crucifixions, but devoid of the reverence of a passion play like Oberammergau. They are hideous affairs. A scapegoat allegedly volunteers to save his soul and portray Christ, carrying a heavy wooden cross in the inevitable procession while everyone throws stones at him, beats him and inflicts every other imaginable and unimaginable brutality upon him. And during this bloody business other devotees flay themselves and each other. By Easter morning, the rice paddies are littered with bruised and battered bodies of the "saved".

The more enlightened upper classes limited themselves to an all-day session in church, fasting, – not unlike my Anglican grandmother. Many pay the local convents to go on "retreat". They entered the convent for three or four days before Easter to pray and meditate, but the papers were full of photographs of the lovelier ladies on their knees, or in fetching poses with candles and rosaries, and they were altogether more in the public limelight in so called "retreat" than before.

When Roswell and I were stymied in a traffic jam downtown because of a passing procession for St. Carmen, he asked some of the candle holders:

"Who was she? What did she do?"

They all knew where the procession was going, and the important people participating, and many had taken part in it year after year, but no one could tell us who she was, or what she had done.

* * *

May was our favourite season for parades. For ten days – the length of a novena – little children were chosen as king and queen. A tiny boy wearing a crown and carrying a wooden sword, with his little queen, would be followed by a retinue of symbolic figures such as Justice and the seven virgins. At dusk they carried candles and sang a haunting little song over and over again as they went. In well-off districts, they had bands and rode in jeeps, and their parents were expected to furnish a feast for their neighbours.

Our barrio was too poor for anyone to afford more than rice and salt fish, and the children were usually dressed in paper. They couldn't afford candles, but they picked long stems of papaya, stripped them of leaves and lit them instead. For ten warm soft May evenings we would watch the lighted tapers go past from our verandah. The air would be heavy with the sweet smelling white flowers of sampaquita in the children's wreaths, and we would listen to the hymn accompanied by a lone banjo, sung in the curious timbre that characterises Filipino voices. Roswell would irreverently pick out the little blighters who threw stones at our dogs pretending to be angels, but it was one procession that really moved us.

We were so very happy in our little house. Fond as we might be of friends, throughout our lives we were always happiest alone together. It never occurred to me that during the daytime, when Roswell and Gerardo had left for work, I was totally alone in an alien environment. I was as isolated as the women of the early

American settlers in the Western movies and in just about as primitive conditions.

There was a woman living in a shack built almost entirely of cardboard cartons way off on the far side of the cemetery. Sometimes I saw her laundry draped over the stone angels and cherubs to dry, but I never saw her. I asked Gerardo who she was, and he said:

"She is a dirty business woman. No one has any respect for her – a very dirty girl!"

It seemed even here there was a stigma for sexual licence.

I could smell, rather than see, the distant pig farm, and was far apart from the sprawl of nipa huts behind us that made up the barrio.

On our arrival, one old lady presented herself as "lavendera". She was fat and smiling, but didn't look very clean. Gerardo called her simply "the old woman", and told us she supplied the barrio with tuba – a local beer brewed from coconuts. She pointed to my ungainly pregnant stomach and with a broad smile rubbed her own and said:

"Very painful!"

That was the extent of our conversation, but I had long overcome my alarm in Calcutta of language barriers. In the Philippines, and later in China, smiles and laughter were almost as effective as words. We had to dispense with her as lavendera. Like Severo at Valenzuela, she ministered to her own family and friends. We never seemed to have anything clean. Yet we remained smiling friends, and in the days of the flood she literally swam through the waters to us. News of an American couple living in a barrio must have raced along the native grapevine, but Roswell's FLC work had helped so many ordinary Filipinos, and Gerardo was our ambassador, that our barrio was friendly. Always the threat came from outside.

* * *

The little house had one raised floor, and we used to drive the car underneath. The dogs and ourselves lived over it. One night, when we were asleep in bed, I was awoken by an unusual noise. I heard something moving around underneath us. I woke up Roswell and said:

"Something's going on!"

We sat up in bed and listened. Kali and her puppies were sound asleep. Everything seemed quiet. Roswell said:

"You've been dreaming. Go back to sleep!"

In the morning when he went down to the car to go to work, the front two wheels and tyres were missing. It was propped up on stones. The car had been manually lifted and the wheels unbolted. My voice must have alerted the thieves, and they had left with the job unfinished. So much for our watchdogs.

Roswell notified the Police, who said it was a common occurrence. The best we could do was to go to the market on the far eastern side of the city, and, if we were lucky, we might find the wheels, rims and tyres on sale there and buy them back. He did just that, at considerable cost.

* * *

Miles Timber was a curious company of people. Born of Pete's Palawan dream, which had so captivated Roswell, it had to draw on whoever Pete could find for capital and backing. Roswell had managed to interest two brothers he had met with Eugenio Lopez. They were the Misa brothers from one of the old Spanish families, and they had another brother who was Director of Prisons. Roswell and I were invited up country to Bilibid Prison to meet him. We might have been in the old deep south of Dixie, it was so gracious. The Governor lived in a large and lovely Spanish-style house, immaculately tended, and waited on hand and foot by the prisoners. It was hard to believe we were up country adjoining a primitive and probably pretty brutal prison. They were a charming family, and like many rich Filipinos, had been educated in America and embraced the very highest style of living from both worlds. The brothers were interested in exotic hardwoods, mainly, it seemed, to supply their brother with choice logs he put his prisoners to carving and furniture-making for his own gain and to bestow gifts on his friends, including President Roxas. Charming as the set-up was, it didn't seem right that the whole penal undertaking was run as a soft option for the Misas, but Roswell said:

"The prisoners probably get a better deal working for him than being put to the equivalent of rock-breaking, whatever that is Filipino style".

But it was the Luzon Stevedoring Co who furnished most of the backing and equipment of the enterprise, and they were a very rough outfit. There was also Lefty, the enormous negro who managed Pete's steam laundry, and his friend Harrigan, also a very large man. Harrigan was a coarse, red-headed Irish/American who had been shipped from the West coast of the US to the Philippines to help in US timber operations before the Japanese invasion. He was a hard drinker and a fighter, and had had brushes with the Police in the US as well as locally. He had a mean reputation but unpleasant as he could be, he was said to be an excellent boss in arranging technical matters to get timber out of forests.

"Everyone is so darned scared of him, he can make them do anything!" was Roswell's verdict. But he was a friend of Lefty, and fitted Pete's bill. When the legal details incorporating Pete and the various administrators were drawn up, Harrigan's name had gone down as 'Director'. Roswell imagined this was to make up the legal number of directors needed but couldn't conceive he would be used otherwise, and forgot it.

As with most things, oil petroleum products were very scarce. The only diesel oil was on the black market, probably stolen from ships. Then Shell Oil Company announced they had a shipment of so many thousand gallons and they would allocate it based on need. There would be plenty of unscrupulous customers who would undoubtedly make a good thing out of it by re-selling. The whole city buzzed with excitement. We had tractors and other uses for diesel, but, waiting on the pier, we were not using them at the time, so Roswell did not make any request. He then heard through the grapevine that a large requirement had been put in for Miles Timber.

Roswell was furious, and he went straight to John Sanguinetti, our Shell Company friend we had met over the puppies. Pete was out of town and the request had been signed by Harrigan as 'Director'. He explained the situation, and John thanked him. On the day of the allocation there was no oil for Miles Timber.

When Harrigan found out, his true nature erupted. Fighting mad, he told his drinking associates he would "get that son of a bitch, Bradley!" He got Lefty to find out where we were living and drive him out to us.

They drove up to our gate in a jeep. Harrigan got out and came shouting to the bottom of the steps that led to our verandah, red-headed, red-faced, huge and very ugly. We had been sitting on the verandah. Quite calmly, Roswell told me to go inside with the baby, and he confronted Harrigan at the top of the steps. Harrigan yelled that he had interfered with his right as a director and he was going to take him apart in a lot of unpleasant ways, working himself into a mad frenzy. Roswell's calm simply made him madder. Without raising his voice, Roswell could make his voice carry, and he coldly countered that while not a director he was a good friend of Pete and knew that having nothing to do with the rat race for diesel now would work to the company's advantage in the long run. All this time, hearing a strange voice, the dogs were scratching at the screen door and barking to get out. Lefty called something we couldn't hear from the jeep. Harrigan turned, joined him, and they drove off.

It had been a very nasty situation. We were no longer under the protective umbrella of the State Department and mayhem and murder were every day occurrences. But so was rabies. The dogs had probably saved us. When Pete returned, he reassured Roswell, and we heard no more from Harrigan.

* * *

However, there were other threats. From the start, FLC relations with the Chinese had always been delicate. Helped in the past, the Nationalists had asked for military aircraft, and Roswell had to tell them he wasn't empowered to supply any. They reacted with anger and resentment. Later on he helped them with repairs and spares, and relations became a little less strained.

By autumn 1947, due to Maoist advances east, their headquarters had been pushed to Nanking. Roswell was asked to go up there to give help with certain instruments which would previously have been handled by FLC. They showed Roswell a sketch of a handsome single-storey construction, and told him:

"This will be the future home for the technical side of our Air Force, and will house the engine overhaul and repair plant your Government has given us".

"Oh," said Roswell, "and when do you anticipate its completion?"

"We are confident it will be in operation by February."

"So," wisecracked Roswell, "just about in time for the Reds to march in and take the whole damned thing!".

There was silence.

Afterwards, a colonel with whom he had become friends who had had some education in the US, asked him:

"For God's sake, why in hell did you make a remark like that?"

"Well, I thought it was true!"

"It was a pretty silly thing to say to these people. You are not in your own country now. You cannot possibly understand the mentality and sensitivity of the Chinese. This is a foreign country and we have different ways of doing things. I must tell you. You could be in serious physical danger. I like you and I am deeply concerned."

Roswell asked: "Well, is there anything I can do?"

"Just keep quiet and pray to your God that nothing will happen, but remember we Chinese have long memories!"

Roswell's judgment as to the time of the Reds arriving was right to within a matter of days. Without a shot being fired, they walked into Shanghai and took over the whole operation, but his tactless remark had added a second threat to that from the defeated Leyte Supply syndicate. Now, as freelance individuals with a baby in our family, we had less protection and more to lose.

* * *

Departures from Manila airport were no secret, and, as soon as Roswell had taken off, the news circulated that his family were alone in the barrio. Jimmy Lambert, working there, had his ear to the grapevine and there was very little that went on he didn't know about. Of course, Roswell had asked him to look out for me, but not with any concrete fear. It was only for a few days, and Gerardo would be home each night.

Roswell's "Look out for them!" was as routine as Jimmy's "Have a good trip!"

Nevertheless, being Manila, Jimmy did look out.

At that time of the year, the great heat of the day falls suddenly when the sun goes down. I could look out over the cemetery and almost see the change of temperature as the sun in a great red ball started to descend. A tropical sunset is like a huge sigh of the universe – unbelievable depth of vibrant colour and fire exhaling, gathering and expending itself into cool shade. I loved to watch it.

The second night of Roswell's trip, Caleb was asleep in his little meat safe bed, and as I looked out watching the sight of the sun going down, lazily I noticed a small group of men silhouetted against the sky down by the pig pen area. They didn't seem to belong to our barrio, but I wasn't overly interested or concerned.

Suddenly, there was a skidding of tyres and brakes and a jeep clattered up to our gate with two armed men in it. Out leapt Jimmy Lambert, gun at the ready, shouting:

"Don't ask questions – get yourself and the baby into this jeep as fast as you can!"

Momentarily stunned, I said something about:

"What about the dogs?"

"They'll be OK – get into the jeep – hurry up!"

Caleb was lying in his nappy. I clutched a handful more, and scooping him up, ran out. The dogs were barking. The wakened baby started to cry, and Jimmy pushed me into the jeep behind himself and the driver, telling me to

"Hang on!"

The jeep swung around and screeched into action. It was desperately uncomfortable as I hung onto the baby and the metal sides of the jeep, and bumped in and out of potholes and lumps in the road, all the time growing cooler. I struggled to cover Caleb with the extra nappies. Nothing much was said until we got to Jimmy's house in Makati, after an hour's cold, bruising and frightening ride. Cherie, Jimmy's Mestiza wife, rushed out to embrace us with all the warmth of her Spanish forebears, practically carrying us inside to be fussed over.

Everything had happened so fast and so violently. They all seemed to know more about what was happening than I did. With Roswell gone, Jimmy had got wind of a plot to kidnap Caleb and myself – an all too common occurrence – and was convinced the group of men I had seen by the pig pen were the would-be abductors. There had been no time to dally with explanations. He had rescued us just in time. Next day an escort would take me out to oversee the dogs, but until Roswell returned I was to stay with them, and the whole household set about indulging me. A bed was made up on the small verandah, screened against mosquitoes, but it was open to the weather on three sides, and during the night a wind got up. This, combined with our frantic dash in the jeep in cooling temperature, combined to give Caleb a severe chill, and he quickly became a very sick baby. I had only Cherie to turn to, who was hopeless. With great heart, she suggested grinding little geckos (lizards) and other native remedies. I was desperate.

By the time Jimmy got home from work, the situation was serious. Rather over-fortified with drink, he set off to find a European doctor and knocked into a wall, but finally he returned late at night with a very dirty old German who had definitely seen better days. To my horror, he snatched Caleb from my arms by his heels and thrust a filthy finger down his throat. The baby gagged. A thick cord of mucus started to come out of his mouth. He undoubtedly saved his life, but it couldn't have been more primitive.

When Jimmy took us to meet him at the airport, Roswell hardly recognised the poor little chap; he had lost so much weight and was so poorly. He gradually picked up again, but he was always a delicate little boy.

* * *

It was now my turn for tribulation. After a painful bout of milk fever, I managed to feed Caleb for eight months, which was a blessing. The only milk available, other than carraboa, was in tins at the US commissary. But home again in the barrio, I came down with a terrible dose of yaws.

Filipinos call this foul disease "galese". You break out in disgusting ulcers. The running sores bore deep inside you and send agonising pains into your glands. I had them on my legs, with shooting pains into my groin. In the accepted way, Gerardo boiled tea from guava leaves, and Roswell, nursing me with unfailing tenderness, used it to clean pus and bathe my repulsive sores, before putting on casla tree juice. This momentarily formed scabs, but germs multiplied underneath and began to eat great holes. I was nearly insane with agony. Roswell had to care for Caleb, and in such a moment the dogs, who had whined and acted distressed, came and licked my ulcerating festers. It was extraordinary but their hot tongues afforded me some relief, perhaps by keeping the sores open, but I became very ill. Roswell fetched Dr. Fletcher all the way from Manila. He scraped off scabs and dabbed on peroxide and gentian violet, but there wasn't much more he could do.

And then the islands received their first shipment of penicillin. My leg was saved. After daily shots, I recovered, but it had been a bad time, and being so ill my milk was drying up. This meant an unhappy baby. Yet again the dogs came to our rescue.

This time it was the puppy Magnesia. While I was carrying Caleb, this little dog had been very close to me, and actually had a false pregnancy herself. I had put Caleb into a little playpen Roswell had made him from wooden slats, and left him grizzling because he wasn't properly fed. I was nearly in tears myself, when suddenly there was peace. I stole back to see if he was asleep and could hardly believe it. Magnesia had wriggled through the slats of the pen, positioned him with her nose, and was actually feeding him. This created a bond between them which was extraordinary. She was always on guard for him and never allowed any Filipino or Chinese nearer than so far, not even Gerardo. She supplemented me until Caleb was weaned, but he was always her baby.

* * *

Jimmy Lambert had a Chinese friend with a son working in the San Luis Bakery in Manila. Overall, Chinese were not liked by Filipinos. They were clean and hardworking. They all stuck together and had quickly gained a monopoly of the trades and businesses – a parallel to the Jew in Europe – and Filipino resentment showed in current legislation swelling with new laws restricting Chinese enterprises. Mr. Kwong was ambitious for Schio and asked Jimmy if he could find a US household where he might work in return for board and English lessons. Gerardo wanted to go home to Cebu for Christmas, so we agreed to take Schio while he was away. He was a great surprise and illustrated the Chinese/Filipino divide.

Schio was short and thin and looked like a child, but was in fact as old as I was. He had thick coarse black hair, a high pitched voice, and he smelt exquisitely of expensive soap.

"Ah," commented Gerardo, "he uses very much better soap than you or the Colonel!".

Spotless in white pants, with a creaseless white shirt hanging outside, which, in the heat, must have meant several changes a day, his manners were impeccable, and after Gerardo he was like a little atom bomb. How could we help liking anyone so willing? Gerardo would do anything we asked but, sensibly in the heat, he would take his time. His great phrase was "bye and bye", which could mean days. Schio created constant work. Gerardo, used to our US regime, believed in equality, and never had any qualms about announcing a meal with "Chow's up!" Schio would come tiptoeing up to us with a bow that nearly bumped his head on the floor, and with sweeping arm gestures beg us to take refreshment.

"I feel I ought to dress for dinner!" was Roswell's reaction. Roswell bought him a primer, and I drew pictures underneath the translations because he was too embarrassed to read them with us. Progress was difficult because he would never admit he didn't understand, so I never knew if he was following or not. Probably not.

Christmas came. A delivery van from the San Luis Bakery arrived full of extravagant gifts. There were tins of fruit cakes, beautifully iced cakes, boxes of Chinese sausages, and dried lychees and nuts, a bottle of whiskey and calendars. All the calendars were emblazoned with "SAN LUIS BAKERY". One had a pin-up girl in a bathing suit caught by a fishing hook with the caption "NICE CATCH!" Another showed a child with a chicken and all the bakery's specialities – "SAN LUIS BAKERY – WE ACCEPT ORDERS FOR CAKES, COOKIES, ETC" across it. Schio pinned them all up around the walls, like Oriental Christmas cards. We couldn't hurt his feelings by taking them down, so for the length of his stay, to our friends' amazement, we became an advertising agent for San Luis Bakery. With enormous goodwill on both sides – certainly great generosity and effort from Schio – I feel we let him down. He mastered very little English. He couldn't eat our food. Worst of all, in expecting him to care for our dogs, I fear he lost face. Never is a hopeless word, but maybe Kipling was right. East and West don't meet. We were greatly relieved when Gerardo returned.

* * *

Even at this late date, US Army surplus was still being found on the various island bases. Over 1,000 aluminium propeller blades were brought to Manila. Miles Timber bought them. A group in FEATI with money to invest wanted to buy them to make pots and pans. Pete was thrilled. But Roswell looked them over and thought they were too heavy for aluminium. He suspected they had been hardened with something to temper and strengthen them, so he wrote to the Aluminium Company of America and asked them. They promptly confirmed that various other metals had been included to make a high grade quality, and stressed that under no circumstances should they be used to make pots and pans, because in cooking it would contaminate the food. Risking everyone's wrath, he told the buyers and suggested they sell them on for building construction. This they did very well.

"That hunch saved a lot of Filipinos from being poisoned!" he said, and this time everyone was pleased. I doubted if any of the others would have risked jeopardising the sale by coming clean over the aluminium, and looking with pride at his beloved face, I felt sure he knew it too. Had it not ended well, would we have had another visit from Harrigan and Lefty?

Meanwhile, all had gone ahead on Palawan. We had orders for logs for several shipments. Wireless reports through Luzon Stevedoring Co grew daily more exciting, and finally we heard a barge was loaded and ready to move. We were confident of success at last.

What we had not taken into account were acts of God.

* * *

After the heat of the long summer, we were on the edge of the typhoon season. We had suffered unrelenting monsoon. Rain stormed down in sheets without break. The air steamed, opening every pore in our bodies and sucking out all energy. Our very skins felt sticky and in the all-pervading damp, even clothes and towels were moist. Leather grew mould within hours. We couldn't hear ourselves speak above the thunder of the rain, and it made a deafening bombardment on our corrugated tin roof.

And then real disaster arrived. A terrific hurricane came up from Borneo and hit the islands with merciless force. There were earth tremors, constant thunder and lightning, terrific gusts of wind over 100mph, and always unquenchable rain. In Manila, the Tondo and all the low slum areas, where poorer families crowded into flimsy shacks made from cardboard and loose boxes, hundreds were drowned. In Bulacan, the fish ponds were simply washed away. The pavements in Iloilo cracked into craters. Everywhere crops were lost, and the hardship was endless. It was the very worst typhoon disturbance for thirty years, and the loss of life and property was tremendous.

In our barrio, all the nipa huts blew down. Our house still stood, but like a boat at sea. All the ground around, including our car beneath us, was under water. The cat, too scared of the dogs to come inside, hung by its claws to the mosquito screening but we couldn't reach it. In a matter of hours, there wasn't a tombstone to be seen in the submerged cemetery, and the only landmarks were the tops of a few tall mango trees.

But, as ever, oriental resilience came to the fore. The barrio people took to the waters like mariners. They set out on upturned tables, or hastily made rafts of fallen banana trunks, to salvage what they could from the floating debris of loose household equipment, brooms and brushes and even the old woman's empty tuba-beer barrels. A heavy pig up the lane had been drowned, and, always ready to turn every occasion into a money-making event, they ferried from rooftop to rooftop selling hunks of pork. The old woman's shack was submerged but she had managed to tie her two pigs to a door and hoist them up onto the roof, but a great many drowned animals floated by.

The waters, which had risen overnight, subsided as rapidly, revealing devastation. Where before there had been a wooden shack, there was now nothing. A few boards and the roof were flat on the mud a good hundreds yards on. Banana trees had been uprooted and were lying in exhausted heaps in strange places. Our custard-apple tree lay across the gate, and we saw our papaya with its three precious fruit crash to its death, along with a promising crop of unripe mangoes and our only banana bunch. We had long ago run out of dry nappies for Caleb. I was ready to weep, but, as Roswell pointed out, we were so much better off than our neighbours, whose good nature never deserted them, and as the waters receded, he triumphantly caught a large stranded fish in the garden for supper.

A few days later, a Government official called to take loss statistics.

"Any damage, missus?" he asked.

I launched into details of the waterlogged car, sodden ammunition boxes, the waterlogged treasures of the basement.

"Such is of no interest, missus," he reproved me. Smiling broadly, he announced:

"I have come to know how many deaths!"

* * *

Of course, our main concern was what had happened on Palawan. It took several days before we got wireless contact – a report of the greatest catastrophe. They had experienced a terrific downpour with a rising wind which, after dark, grew to such intensity that the shelters constructed for the work crews were totally destroyed. Huge waves surged up and washed the loaded barge loose, and then, with a wind change, turned it back towards the pier, where it bounced against the piles and began to demolish it. The derrick was blown over and sank. Eventually the whole pier fell, and the cargo of logs was washed away, strewn along the beach for over a mile. It was the deathblow to a dream.

"But we lived that dream," said Roswell, "and what an adventure!" He always knew that sooner or later we should have to return to America. He no longer had any Government position or income. We wanted more babies, and the Philippines was no place to raise children. The time had come to move on.

There remained just one last source of business for the Leyte Supply Co Roswell was handling for the imprisoned Khoongs. Philippine Air Lines (PAL), who had had several C47s from FLC in the past, now bought out Don Fernando Sycip's airline (CATC) and they needed several million dollars worth of spares. Leyte Supply still had plenty. Roswell offered them a list with suggested prices. PAL wanted immediate delivery but they couldn't pay the full amount at one time. Jimmy Lambert and Hank Meider, who were now with PAL, came to our aid. They worked out with the PAL financial people that if they could pay 25%, the rest could follow at specified dates. It was then put to PAL that the way the matter had been handled was in large part due to Roswell, who was not an officer but merely helping the owners, and so he was entitled to a commission. They agreed. Both PAL and FEATI had weekly DC3s flying to San Francisco, and they also offered the three of us a free flight home.

However, this was our last chance to see China, at a unique time in its history. It would be the last time we should see Chinese friends. Above all, Roswell wanted to see Lawrence Kwong.

In the 1900s, the Chinese had sent their first students to be educated in America. Roswell was eleven years old and met Kwong who was at Yale. Kwong took him camping and taught him to cook and shoot and fish, and quickly became his boyhood hero. Thirty years later, when he got to Manila, he was able to find him again through Yale alumni, but it was difficult. Now they were both Air Force colonels on what was to be opposing sides. Kwong was with Chang Kai Shek on Formosa (Taiwan) and they could only manage short clandestine visits in Shanghai.

The other friend was Khe Ling Yui (Kal). As young men, Kal and Roswell had started together, in 1926, with the Bankers Trust Co in New York. They had kept in touch and now Kal was a wealthy businessman. In true Chinese fashion, he embraced us as family and offered his home as ours.

Once again, Jimmy Lambert came to our aid. He changed our flight itinerary to start from Shanghai instead of Manila. He flew us up himself to save us fares, leaving us for a few days in Hong Kong while he went en route to Formosa. It was perfect.

* * *

We were very sad to leave our little house, where we had experienced so much happiness and adventure. It had been a fairytale time. At the moment of our leaving, there was a second when time stood still. I knew nothing would be quite the same again. It had been our first wonderful time to be alone with ourselves – our own first home – our first baby – and a great adventure. There would be more babies, and Roswell would make whatever lay ahead glorious for me, but I should never see Gerardo again, and that virginal first-time quality would have gone. The world would intrude on us and make us part of it, and there was nothing I could do to stop it.

8

HONG KONG

Helped by an offshore wind, Jimmy put us down on the Kowloon airstrip, and Herbert and Pauline, Roswell's Chinese Air Force friends, met us and booked us into a small waterside hotel. It was spotless, with taps that ran water, and baths, and electric light, and, best of all after our tropical heat, cool breathable air. Second floor up, we breakfasted on a tiny balcony overlooking a busy harbour packed with small boats moving in and out between ocean liners and Naval vessels. Dozens of these sampans were jammed together as houseboats for entire families with all their dogs and cats and poultry. They were so close people moved from one to another, and they seemed to be cooking all day. In one corner, at low tide, they pulled the boats up and lit fires under them to dry them off.

* * *

Early evening on our second day, there was a terrific clamour from these sampans. It sounded like machine guns, and lights shot up like star shells. This spread to the Naval vessels further out, who staged a wonderful display with real rockets. It was a general celebration. The sampans were exploding fireworks in Chinese

Hong Kong

Aberdeen

Herbert and Pauline Yuan

Left and Below
The Floating Restaurants

fashion. In England, Princess Elizabeth had given birth to a son, and Hong Kong was greeting a future Prince of Wales. I'm glad they didn't know that one day he would have to hand them all back to China.

Herbert and Pauline paid us a great honour by taking us into their home. The Chinese usually entertain foreigners in restaurants. They had a tiny baby with an amah squeezed into a little box of a flat, its floor space probably no larger than a sampan, with the laundry line slung out of the window. It was an eye-opener to see such cramped quarters allotted to an Air Force Major, but it was the tone of Hong Kong, bursting with a multitude of people all jostling for insufficient space.

Hong Kong seemed to be endlessly celebrating carnival, its streets hung with colourful banners and full to bursting with busy chattering people. There were shops that mirrored London, and we bought Caleb, who until now had only worn a nappy, his first pair of shoes and woolly pants and sweater. We rode the funicular to the Peak, where once only Europeans had been allowed to live, and had a marvellous view of the teeming city and harbour. We drove to Aberdeen, a fishing village famous for its floating restaurants. Local boatwomen, in the ubiquitous grass hats and blue pants and jacket, competed to ferry customers, with a lot of good-natured banter, in their unsteady little craft out to the anchored restaurant ships, where you selected live fish still swimming in tanks to be caught, cooked and served for your supper. We went to Repulse Bay and its gigantic hotel and beach, which might have been the French Rivera. Nearby, an extraordinary building had the legend that should its owner stop building, he would die, so he just went on endlessly adding to it until the war forced him to stop. He was then quite old, and he died. Then on to Stanley camp, where the British had been interned, and home through Shankiwan in the dark. And everywhere we carried little Caleb like a parcel.

It was an extraordinary few days between the Eastern and Western worlds, full of colour and noise and frenetic activity.

9

SHANGHAI

Jimmy arrived back from Formosa and flew us up to Shanghai. Kal met us, and took us out to his beautiful home on the Hungjao Road in a very plush part of Shanghai in the international settlement. We were greeted with bows and giggling smiles, but no English, by his kind motherly wife and five of his children. Roswell had warned me that he also had a concubine with two more children, but she lived elsewhere.

"She's an awful woman," he said. "I can't think what Kal was up to, and I hope we don't see her!" We didn't.

Kal had built the large Spanish-style house in the 1930s in a 5-acre landscaped garden of shrubs and trees and water. There was a hump-backed bridge in white marble, and huge pieces of lava-like rock lying around in the shrubs and chrysanthemums. But less than a yard from the end of the house was a huge unsightly mound. He explained that this was the tomb of a man who had died at least a century ago, but the old law stipulated that to move a tomb you must have the permission of all his descendants, which would run into thousands, so he had to build around it.

At the time his mother was still alive, and it was tradition that he support her for the rest of her life, so he had added a self-contained annex. Now he took us there, and said:

Hungjao Road, Shanghai

Kal and family

Our annexe of the house

The Garden

"This is yours for as long as you wish!"

And so the three of us moved in, and it was like living in a luxury hotel. We slept in the annex, and ate with the family. There were plenty of servants but we seldom saw one. At meals they simply brought on the main dishes, and Madame Yui served.

During our first meal there was a large platter of flat fish, like a turbot. Madame Yui carefully separated the long curved bones and skin and innards of the fish into two separate bowls before serving portions of the delicious white meat into the rest. To our amazement, the skin and bone bowls were given to Roswell and me. Kal steadfastly stared at the ceiling, and the elder daughter, Jean, the only one who spoke English and knew Western ways, kept her eyes on the tablecloth. Alongside the chopsticks, thoughtfully, we had been given a knife and fork. Rather abashed, we went to pick up the cutlery. Kal and Jean exploded with laughter, spluttering Chinese to Madame Yui. We were told to pass our bowls back, and then given a normal serving.

"You were honoured!" Kal explained. "As guests you were given the choicest portions. We like the skin and bones better than the fish itself as they have all the flavour. My wife thought she was giving you the most desirable piece of the fish!"

The Chinese love children, and Caleb's golden hair entranced them. The first thing the Yuis did was outfit him in Chinese toddler's clothes. Made of padded cotton, they have the trousers slit underneath and up the back, with the two sides overlapping. They part when the baby squats, cleverly dispensing with Western style nappies.

But there was one urgent problem, and that was getting him milk. With no cows in Shanghai, the only source was tins in the open market, but everything was in short supply. A servant had to get there in the early hours of the day and queue for one tin, and this was punctured with a questionably clean skewer before being handed over to stop hoarding. We could only hope it was alright.

We had chosen a terribly anxious time to see Shanghai. As we arrived, martial law was imposed and a curfew came into effect. Everywhere there was general unrest. The shops were empty, and there were queues for blocks and blocks from the early hours for rice that just wasn't there, resulting in riots. Contributing to the unrest was the terrible poverty of hundreds of thousands of unemployed workers, increasing food shortages, and the inflation and the shrinkage of foreign exchange values which rendered the gold yuan worthless. We heard the FLC office had alerted all US citizens and had an evacuation ship at the ready. But the Yuis insisted we stayed on and royally cocooned us. Kal was determined to show us all he could.

Madame Yui kept a shrine in the house to honour departed ancestors, dressing the household Gods in red paper and tending it daily, burning incense sticks with little bowls of offerings. We already knew the reverence the Chinese paid to their ancestors from Manila, and that their burial would be as elaborate as the relatives could afford, but now in Shanghai thousands couldn't afford a funeral at all. Not only girl babies but bodies of all ages were a common sight floating down the Whanpoo river to the sea. In the country, on open spaces beside streams, the dead were parked in rough unnamed boxes with no identification at all.

Another growing custom was when someone fell ill, or was dying, his family took him to the city, laid him on newspapers on the sidewalk by the side of a building, usually with a tin can of water, and left him to die. In the morning, the usual dawn police patrol would find him and he would be taken away for free by the authorities. We found this most distressing, but Kal strongly warned Roswell never to interfere.

Once when Kal was driving us up a main street, we were stopped by a collision ahead between a rickshaw and a bicycle. The cyclist was lying in the street, badly hurt. Instinctively, Roswell opened the door to go his aide, but Kal grabbed him and said fiercely:

"Get back! Don't go near that man!"

"What the heck!" said Roswell, "can't you see he's in agony?"

Kal simply repeated, "Don't do it!", and hung onto him. He later explained that should Roswell have helped him and he died, or was in any way incapacitated, he, Roswell, would be responsible for looking after him and his dependants until he died. That was the custom.

* * *

'Gwilos' (foreign devils or barbarians), as Westerners were called, were rare in a Chinese home and to enjoy us Kal invited a special friend. He was an Englishman, who, many years ago, had come to China with the Foreign Office. His tour of duty ended, he stayed on, married a Chinese girl, and lived happily ever after. He was now very old, blue-eyed and gentle. I was seated next to him at lunch. We talked about England, now so different to what he remembered. I asked him where he came from and he said Yorkshire. Leaning over, he patted my hand in a grandfatherly fashion, and said:

"I can see you walking your dogs on the moors with the wind in your hair!"

For a moment he was in an idyllic other side of the world.

"I have no regrets – China is my country now – but looking at you I think of daffodils!"

I thought of the homesick young lieutenant in Bangkok who had said the same thing. Daffodils are fresher than roses.

When he left, he made his farewells to the Yuis in the accepted manner, then he just took my hand and with a nod said very softly:

"Thank you!"

I felt honoured. Somehow it was his final goodbye to England. Kal and Roswell were smiling. We all knew. I hoped I had been the ambassadress that Granny would have wished.

The Khoong family wanted to wine and dine us but all the restaurants were closed. Hotels would only serve residents. However, Ed Khoong took us to a party at the Mandarin Club – a very select little place furnished as an old-time Mandarin palace, dimly lit with dozens of paper lanterns hanging from it's ceiling like chandeliers. We danced to a one-man Filipino band, and the food was marvellous. Outside people were starving. In spite of their padded clothes, they looked thin and the rickshaw coolies were ragged and barefoot in the intense cold. I hated the thought of having one pull me, but Roswell pointed out:

"He wants to. The fare will put rice in his bowl".

The one person Roswell really wanted to see was Lawrence Kwong but it was difficult and he could only manage a few short visits. Both his mother's and his father's family had held Mandarin rank at the court of the old Empress. He had been one of the first Chinese children to be educated in America, and spent his life later in the mining industry until he got mixed up in the Jap war. He was now an Air Force colonel for Chang Kai Shek at a time when it was dangerous to have Nationalist sympathies. He came to the Yui house several times, but we didn't want to endanger Kal. It was very emotional. He and Roswell reminisced over their days in America with deep affection, and I could see why. They were both such admirable, loveable men. Kwong had lost his first wife and most of his children through war, or tuberculosis, but the final blow had been the loss of his second young wife, and I know he was happy for Roswell that he had me – and a son.

* * *

A day or so before we left, Kal took us shopping. We had seen porcelain rice bowls in lovely colours and design at almost gift prices. I dearly wanted some rice-pattern cups – the typical 3-piece of lid, cup and saucer, in blue and white with translucent patterns where rice grains had been impressed and then burnt out by firing.

Our money was in American Express cheques and Kal managed to exchange $125 for us. It came in various denominations from 500 to 1,000 – in all over one million CNC, and filled up an attaché case, packed tight, with still a bundle left. We cleared out a space under the seat of Kal's jeep to take the attaché case, and divided up the remaining bundle between Kal and Roswell's pockets and my shoulder bag.

On the way we visited a Buddhist temple, crossing a wide canal by some shallow wooden steps shaped like a humpbacked

Shanghai - 1946

The Two Colonels - Kwong and Roswell

bridge, going up and down. As we went down, we passed a little Chinese girl sitting on one side of the steps. She was neatly dressed, with a bowl of rice on her lap, apparently asleep.

The temple approach was crowded with merchants selling everything from fantailed goldfish, canaries and little wild birds, to jars of snakes to grind up to sustain virility and give a man a son, professional fortune-tellers, scribes with little tablets and ink blocs who would write letters for you, barbers, tooth-pullers, a mass of people all talking at once. Inside, the temple was mostly a series of dark dirty little rooms, each with a statue of a Buddha and places for incense sticks and dishes of offerings. In a large room, young monks were reading and reciting all at once, and going about their ceremonial duties. The impression was dirt and confusion.

We came out into a street of porcelain shops, and with Kal's help picked out some lovely bowls and the rice-pattern teacups. We were attended by the entire family of the shop owner, and offered glasses of boiling water. They made endless little changes to the list we had selected and eventually presented the total at the present rate of exchange. This had altered during the day to our disadvantage, and our mass of paper money was now nowhere near enough. We had to leave half the bowls behind.

Walking back to the jeep, we re-crossed the humpbacked bridge over the canal. There, quite unmoved, was the little girl we had seen before, still asleep, but the bowl of rice was black with flies, and we realised that she was dead. It was a sign of the times, and left a sad memory.

* * *

Every day of our stay, the Communist forces had been growing nearer. Already there had been a great exodus of wealthy people with Nationalist sympathies. The time had come for us to leave. We were very touched that so many Chinese friends turned out in the early morning to see us off. We all knew it would be the last time we should see each other. This was particularly affecting with Kal, but most of all with Kwong, for whom we now both had so much affection.

The airport was crowded. Within the past forty-eight hours, as the war news came in from the interior, new rules had come into effect. We were strictly limited in weight to a medium-sized suitcase, and there would be rigid customs examinations on entering Hong Kong. We saw well-dressed women with short sleeves, or bare arms, wearing up to eight wrist watches and jewelled bracelets, as if showing these valuables the balance of their luggage would pass without trouble. Passports and documents were examined several times, and there seemed endless formalities to be observed before we could board the plane.

At the last moment, we were called out before a young man. He took our papers and was arrogant and critical, making all sorts of objections and threats and being generally obnoxious. Roswell was no longer a US official. We were getting nowhere and there was nothing he could do about it. It looked as if we were going to be detained, and alongside his anger I could tell he was alarmed. I felt sick remembering the Chinese threats of his past.

And then Kwong appeared. He had heard the unpleasant language and asked:

"What is the matter? Are you in trouble?"

The customs youth said nothing but Roswell explained that he was finding all kinds of objections to our passports, which were completely in order. Kwong turned to the customs man and let out a string of Chinese. The youth wilted visibly. Immediately his attitude changed. He scribbled the necessary on our documents, and off we went to the plane.

* * *

It was a fearful flight. As soon as we had taken off, the cockpit was locked in case of a highjack, and the nervousness of the passengers was very apparent. A young Chinese couple sitting in front of us had a tiny baby. After an hour or so into the flight, the baby began to cry. Its father was embarrassed and scolded the mother, but she couldn't pacify it. Finally the father called the stewardess, who took the baby to the back of the aircraft, and within a few minutes there was silence, but chloroform fumes drifted down to us. It was obvious that the stewardess had given chloroform-soaked pads to the baby to quieten it. Eventually she returned it to the couple, sleeping peacefully, but we trembled throughout the rest of the trip in case Caleb should cry and they forced the same treatment on him.

Hank Meider was our pilot, so we were not alarmed, but as we approached landing time the expected "No Smoking" and "Fasten your Seat Belts" instructions never came. Instead we felt some manoeuvring of the plane, and then Hank announced over the intercom that there was a heavy fog ahead at Kowloon so we were diverting to Canton.

The Flying Cloud airstrip at Canton was very small and there we were stuck. Time passed and we needed food for Caleb but we had no yuan left, and, of course, there was no milk. At once, our fellow passengers, none of whom we knew, scouted around and came up with some soya milk for him. Unfortunately he didn't like it, so I had to drink it to avoid hurting anyone's feelings after such a kind gesture, and mercifully he was content with sucking my finger until he fell asleep. Finally news came that a strong breeze had now cleared the fog at Kowloon, and we could proceed.

Kal's secretary met us at the airport, which was a blessing. The customs regulations were draconian. Luggage was emptied out onto the floor and sieved through for valuables, and detailed medical examinations were taking place. Earlier on we heard that four nuns who had been working in West China had been virtually raped in this procedure. Men and women were separated. To my terror, Caleb and I were pulled from Roswell and herded with all the other women. Somehow Kal's secretary, and a friend of Roswell's from the British Government, rushed to our rescue, and after some very nasty moments we were reunited.

We couldn't get back onto the plane fast enough for Hank to fly us on to Manila. This time there was a full load of mostly US businessmen, or educational people, leaving with their families, many with regret. More and more we realised that it was full time for us all to go home.

* * *

There had been so many wonderful moments. We had learnt so much – had so many thrills –seen such glorious sights – eaten such exotic foods – and made so many friends. Leaving had to hurt.

We were very touched at the crowd of people – Chinese, Filipino, our own and all the rest – who came to see us off. They came to thank Roswell for all he had done, and the way he had done it. We had over-nighted with the Lamberts, and their lavendera had so over-starched my dress I could hardly bend, but if it straightened my backbone, it couldn't hold back my tears. Roswell had arranged for Gerardo to work for PAL and I could see him at the back, standing alone on the tarmac, much like he had on our last day at Valenzuela, but this time we had to leave him. In spite of all the kindnesses and affection we had been given in what is really a cruel country, I minded leaving Gerardo the most.

"Don't be sad!" Roswell said. "We've had a great adventure, but to make one great you have to give your heart. One long flight and there will be another one ahead!"

On our way, we flew over Leyte, once so full of surplus planes and aircraft spares, now empty. Roswell had truly made airlines fly.

POSTSCRIPT

> **"Filipinos cry as airline closes**
> Manila's television stations played John Denver's *Leaving on a Jet Plane* yesterday as Filipinos bid a sad farewell to Philippine Airlines, Asia's oldest.
>
> Flight attendants cried on their last flights after Manolo Aquino, PAL executive vice-president, announced the collapse of talks with PAL's largest union to try to save the ailing company.
>
> Earlier in the day, scores of PAL employees, many dressed in black, held a prayer vigil to "Keep PAL flying" at the domestic airport. The last domestic flight of the 57-year-old airline arrived in Manila from the central city of Cebu. Minutes later, its last international flight left for San Francisco."
>
> AP, Manila
> 24.9.98

Newspaper cutting from Associated Press, 24.9.1998, 57 years after Roswell sold PAL their first plane:

* * *

At time of writing, Cathay Pacific is still flying, 62 years after Roswell sold "the brigand" his first plane.

Throughout, since he seldom used his given name, I have substituted it with that of his great grandfather – Roswell Bradley.